12,99   TS 92/3?

Developing a European Dimension in Primary Schools

Gordon H. Bell

David Fulton Publishers Ltd
London

For Kathy, Nan and Edmund, Catherine and Victoria

David Fulton Publishers Ltd
2 Barbon Close, London WC1N 3JX

First published in Great Britain by
David Fulton Publishers 1991

British Library Cataloguing in Publication Data

Bell, Gordon H. (Gordon Hartley), *1939–*
   Developing a European dimension in primary schools
   I. Title
   372.192

   ISBN 1-85346-170-9

Typeset by Chapterhouse, Formby L37 3PX
Printed in Great Britain by BPCC Wheaton Ltd Exeter

Contents

Preface

> We are not forming coalitions between States, but union among people. When an idea corresponds to the needs of the times, it is no longer the property of those who invented it and is stronger than those responsible for it.
>
> (Monnet, 1978)

Visionary politics, grand designs and great debates necessarily figure in the development of a culture. Today we find ourselves enmeshed in an idea whose logic was forged through two World Wars. One consequence of this inheritance is that it will not easily be relinquished, though it may readily go astray. The main aim of this book, therefore, is to consider what we might mean by the concept of a European dimension in education and to map the uses to which it might be put.

The clear danger presently is that unless practitioners join with policy makers to identify both problems and opportunities in teaching about Europe this idea, like many similar ones before it, will degenerate.

In addressing this challenge, there are lots of pointers to practice that can be drawn upon in order to avoid the trap of re-inventing the wheel. This is the second purpose of this book. The timeliness of a strategy which enables teachers, not just in the U.K. but throughout Europe, to make a contribution to developing the European dimension in the curriculum in schools is never more evident than today as we move towards a Single Market. It has not always been so. The emergence of the ideas and activities explored in the various chapters which follow have had a fragmented and eventful history. Yet their impact on the circumstances in which they were placed have had undeniably profound effects in terms of change and professional development as reported by the schools, individuals and agencies who came into contact with them.

The experience of disseminating these ideas and generating collaborative links with our partners in Europe has been constantly rewarding but it has not been free of feelings of frustration, impatience or isolation. Without the continued assistance of the Commission of the European Communities, the very possibility of a multilateral project to enable participants to work across twelve countries would have been unthinkable. It was therefore an early lesson to come to realise that timescales for the ideas here explored were not to be measured in weeks, months or years. I came to work with colleagues who were content to implement ideas in five and ten year cycles and felt entirely at ease with the thought that they would not personally see them put into practice. Their example was formative.

The origins of this book can be traced to June 1974. The occasion was the first meeting of the Ministers of Education of the (then) nine Member States of the European Community following the U.K.'s entry together with Denmark and Ireland. This meeting led to a policy which included promoting closer relations between educational systems in Europe. Three years later, the first E.C. study visit scheme was announced to encourage contacts between institutions of higher education.

In response to this scheme I submitted a proposal in 1977 to investigate policy and practice in selected teacher training institutions in six Member States. The aim was to evaluate opportunities for future course development in the light of the emergent concept of teacher education in a framework of European co-operation. The outcome of this initiative was a Network of European Teacher Educators drawn from the contacts made during the study visit. With the support of the British Council, the Network held a conference jointly with the University of Antwerp in 1979 and it operated until 1982 when the project reported in chapters one and two began.

By this stage it had become starkly apparent that the needs of primary schools, their pupils, parents and teachers were not being fully met in terms of effective participation. To a lesser, but troubling, degree, this is still true some ten years later, for there appears to be a clear bias in policy making in educational institutions across Europe towards secondary and higher education. This is reflected as much in conditions of service amongst teachers as it is in the assumptions that policy makers make about the training systems that produce them. This situation amounts to bad faith. This bias, I believe, is the single most potent factor in feeding the fatal tendency to generate rhetoric from grand designs. Attitudes and beliefs are formed in primary schools and in the families of their pupils. The remainder is re-education, in a system which in its present form leads inexorably to élitism. In an entirely partial and clearly imperfect way, the personal motivation for this book is grounded in this belief.

The themes I have selected to evaluate this standpoint are drawn from fifteen years experience of working at a variety of levels in all twelve Member States of the European Community. In this context, the term 'primary' is intended to refer to the age range five to thirteen years. But, as chapter three makes clear, developing a European dimension is not in my view defined in these terms but is to be understood in the context of an overriding need to improve the teaching of inter-cultural and international understanding. Such an ambitious goal cannot be achieved without the full support of the school and its community. Chapter four presents an account of managing change in a situation characterised by slender resources, information overload and innovation saturation. In recommending policy development in the framework of a whole school development plan, I have attempted to outline a strategy of managing for change and simultaneously dealing with the potential threat of politicising the curriculum.

The final chapter presents a speculative view of the future for the educational enterprise of U.K. primary schools in a European perspective. It attempts to tackle the so far unspoken assumption that sceptical readers will have posed for themselves as to whether all of this adds up to a more or less specious form of propaganda. It concludes by revisiting the theme that is implied throughout; that inter-cultural pedagogy and the teaching of controversial issues matter.

I came to recognise the prime importance of these concerns through the work of the late Lawrence Stenhouse to whom I owe a debt of gratitude. I also experienced through the practitioners and policy makers with whom I worked a constructive ambiguity between the concepts of 'Teaching about Europe' and 'Being a European'. The ways in which this ambiguity is to be represented through the knowledge and understanding of teachers, parents and pupils is, I venture to hope, the central question that will be posed by the issues raised in the chapters which follow.

It has not been my intention to do anything but, if possible, stimulate thoughts towards the resolution of these issues and the many gaps and inconsistencies that the incompleteness of this book provokes. Whilst I would claim a degree of accuracy in the descriptive commentary provided, I make no claims concerning the validity of the conclusions drawn. My chief concern in writing has been to offer an opportunity for critical dialogue. It is in this sense that I have aimed at prudential judgement and not strayed too far into the groves of academe. In offering such an account of the European dimension I am conscious of a variety of assertions that require justification. However, in presenting a projective theory I do not claim that every particular is correct or that it is necessary to achieve this. My main hope is that the analysis put forward is sufficiently right to disturb habitual thinking and sufficiently clear to outline the advantages and disadvantages of alternative actions.

In adopting this approach, and despite my best endeavours, I am conscious of the possibility of misrepresenting evidence or committing the many people on whose advice and support I have relied to propositions that they would not recognise as their own or to which they may be opposed.

Acknowledgements

In acknowledging this overwhelming debt, it is both impossible and invidious to identify individuals and agencies in addition to those whose work is represented in the text. From a base of four people in 1977, the project, which forms the core of the book, has come to involve several thousand people: pupils, parents, advisers, teachers, trainers, students and others interested in actively contributing towards developing a European dimension in the curriculum of primary schools.

It cannot, however, go unrecognised that were it not for the co-operation of colleagues in the Faculty of Education at Nottingham Polytechnic over the recent past, this account would never have been completed. In these particular circumstances, I have been greatly assisted by my secretary Elsie Blackwell who with characteristic tact, skill and good humour brought innumerable drafts to a point where the author could recognise his own manuscript as a book.

To all these people both named and those who must remain anonymous I offer my sincere thanks. The book stands as a reminder of this co-operation and of the collaborative action and research which was necessary to bring it to reality.

CHAPTER 1

Towards a European Dimension in Education

> While teaching circles in the European Community have little hesitation in acknowledging the need to give Europe a place in education, there are questions, doubts and even some confusion as to how the subject might be tackled. (Commission of the European Communities, 1987)

In discussing the themes of this book with colleagues it has often come as a surprise to discover that European educational policy making has a long history. I shall avoid the temptation of launching into an extended account of treaties, resolutions and directives for these have been effectively described elsewhere.[1] However, such developments have a context and cannot be fully understood without an awareness of their broader institutional origins.

Two main bodies have orchestrated movements towards a common educational policy; the Council of Europe and the Commission of the European Communities. The former institution is currently comprised of twenty-four Member nations and has, throughout its history, repeatedly examined the concept of European understanding and proved itself to be an influential forum for the discussion of European cultural concerns.[2]

As early as 1967 the Council of Europe was initiating projects to identify the essential characteristics of a coherent and integrated educational system. Such a 'contribution to the development of a new education policy' (Council of Europe, 1982) described a pattern of 'consensus, pluralism, and diversity' and its conclusions and recommendations on the adaptation of the school system to the economic and social situation then prevailing identified concerns that might readily be seen as setting the parameters of a European

1

dimension today. For example it refers to contacts between Northern and Southern Europe revealing:

> the unquestionable need for a differentiated approach...the preservation of the cultural heritage, the quality of teaching and levels of attainment, the protection of the school against the onslaught of the economic or social environment, and the protection of the individual against collective anonymity. (Council of Europe, 1982)

More recently, to mark the fortieth anniversary of the Council of Europe in 1989, a programme of new work has been launched in modern languages, history and geography together with the encouragement of activities which provide pupils and teachers with opportunities for direct contact.

The Deputy Director of Education, Culture and Sport, Council of Europe providing a review of the European dimension in schools (Stobart, 1990) traced the impact of recent events in Eastern Europe in bringing about radical changes in the framework of European co-operation and integration. He suggested that for a long time it was seen simply as 'education for reconciliation and better understanding'. It had, however, now become the chief focus of debate. For example, in October 1991, the Standing Conference of the European Ministers of Education will review the consequences for the education of all young people of the momentous changes under way in Europe and indicate what should be the balance between national and European priorities in education.

Turning now to the Commission of the European Communities' work in the field of education, it will be seen from the comprehensive scope of actions outlined in Appendix 1 that its interest has been far from passive, despite education (but not training) being part of the Treaty of Rome. Nevertheless, on account of this founding Treaty and unlike the Council of Europe whose conclusions can only be recommendations, E.C. decisions and directives e.g. on the mutual recognition of qualifications, have had notable effects. This is hardly surprising since the *raison d'être* of the Community is to increase the mobility of people, ideas and products within and between its Member States. Yet its influence in the field, say, of teacher training in the U.K. has been barely discernible until very recently when the final brief to the Committee for the Accreditation of Teacher Education required the development of European Awareness in training programmes.[3]

Two main processes have underpinned the Commission's approach to developing a European education policy; (i) 'The Policy Makers' Forum', assembling leading educational experts and high ranking policy makers with a view to providing policy-oriented advice in order to stimulate national initiatives; (ii) 'Activity-based Projects and Networks' operating on a multilateral basis in which institutions, agencies and individuals from a variety of Member States undertake activities with central co-ordination (Goodson, 1982). The Teaching about Europe in the primary school project (later described) is one example of this latter type. A third process has recently been added following the introduction of Summer Universities for teacher trainers. This has moved Commission activities towards a research and development function through systematic exploration of pedagogical issues.

The idea of a European dimension in education appears for the first time in a Resolution of the Council of Ministers of Education in 1976 when it was agreed to 'give a European dimension to the experience of pupils and teachers in primary and secondary schools in the Community'.[4] Involvement in educational affairs has, however, provided a source of tension for some of the partners in the Community from time to time. This has been particularly evident in those governments like the U.K. who are either net contributors to the E.C. budget or who have sharply defined views on responsibilities that should remain with Member States.[5] Such conflicts of interpretation between what the Commission is competent to do and what remains with Member States to carry out has its expression in the technical term 'subsidiarity' about which there will doubtless be increasingly public debate in the years ahead.

Perhaps the single most influential action taken at Community level on the curriculum of schools and colleges in recent years is the Resolution of Ministers of Education of May 24th 1988 on 'Giving Greater Emphasis to the European Dimension in Education'. The objectives of this Resolution are to strengthen the European dimension in education by launching a series of concerted measures for the period 1988–92 to:

● strengthen in young people a sense of European identity and make clear to them the value of European civilisation and of the foundations on which the European peoples intend to base their development today, that is in particular the safeguarding of the principles of democracy, social justice and respect for human rights (Copenhagen Declaration, April 1978);

● prepare young people to take part in the economic and social developments of the Community and in making concrete progress towards European union, as stipulated in the European Single Act;

- make them aware of the advantages which the Community represents, but also of the challenges it involves, in opening up an enlarged economic and social area to them;
- improve their knowledge of the Community and its Member States in their historical, cultural, economic and social aspects and bring home to them the significance of the co-operation of the Member States of the European Community with other countries of Europe and the world.[6] (Commission of European Communities, 1988)

A report of these measures was agreed to be submitted to the education committee by 30th June 1991. To assist the E.C. to undertake its role, a Task Force for Human Resources, Education, Training and Youth was established in 1989.[7]

Scenarios towards a European curriculum

Tracing the evolution of a common policy towards the European dimension is perhaps best understood through documents prepared for ministerial meetings and actions taken at Commission level, following agreement of the ministers of education meeting in Council.

The first action programmes following the 1976 Resolution were designed to improve comparability between educational systems in Europe and to organise activities that promoted the exchange of experience, for example, short study visits, mobility of teachers and pupils, contacts between teacher training institutions and school activities with a European content. Extended language teaching programmes were also envisaged with the aim of all pupils studying at least one other Community language. The June 1980 general report of the education committee focused on teaching about the European Community and Europe in schools. It emphasised the need to develop an awareness of Europe and the European Community in its historical, geographical and political aspects understood as a perspective introduced into the study of existing subjects. Concerning language teaching, the report advocated the study of two Community languages by pupils in addition to their mother tongue and proposed a five year programme (1981–5) to assist efforts to improve basic training for language teachers. By June 1984, the importance of language teaching in strengthening economic and cultural ties was re-asserted. The objective of pupils acquiring practical knowledge of two languages was clearly established together with the aim of supporting periods of study in Europe for initial and in-service teachers and increasing co-operation between teacher training establishments.

In September 1985, talk of enhancing the European dimension was underpinned by explicitly acknowledging its presence in the curriculum of schools and teacher training courses, by promoting short in-service training seminars for teachers, and by supporting the development of teaching materials.

At the time of writing, neither the contents of the E.C. report expected in 1992 summarising progress made over the past fifteen years, nor more importantly the actions that might flow from it, can be known in advance. Yet certain trends might be anticipated by examining the outcomes of initiatives that have arisen through one or more of the main approaches adopted by the Commission in developing its educational policies. Two examples have been selected to identify broad themes and key issues. The first arises from the policy makers' forum approach in which 80 senior educationalists met with policy makers in Maastricht in the south of the Netherlands in June 1987, to discuss the question of how the European dimension can most effectively be realised in schools and colleges (C.E.V.N.O., 1987). The second example relates specifically to primary and middle schools and represents an 'activity based projects and networks' approach.

The Maastricht conference was particularly influential in that it was informed by a state-of-the-art Commission report on giving greater emphasis to the European dimension. The opening quotation to this chapter is also the opening paragraph of this report. It is significant because it underlines the importance of the current need for promoting debate, supporting exploratory initiatives and testing policy against practice. This Commission report effectively provided for the first time a multi-national interpretation of the European dimension in Member States. It confirmed a predictable variation in custom and practice particularly on the question of how pupils are to be informed of the practical choices which European integration entails. For example, some countries specifically provide for political, social or civics education whilst others do not. Meanwhile it was noted that teachers themselves may differ as to their own beliefs concerning the competence of the Community in educational affairs and as a consequence interpret regulations or guidelines in varying ways.

The scope of variation in practice was described in terms of Germany having precise and agreed statements on 'Europe in Education' whilst in Denmark the adoption of central policy documents was not considered appropriate. The preconditions that need to be satisfied for a common education policy document to arise are considered by the report's authors, to include: a clear commitment to do so among authorities, favourable public opinion, internationalisation of pupils', students' and teachers' experience, and access to relevant information. The report concludes that 'making teachers aware in depth of the "Community" process and devising appropriate teaching material remain the keys to success'. In considering the question 'How can we go further and faster?' the report provides a list of possible and desirable measures at various levels (Appendix 2).

The delegates to the conference responded both to the report and to supplementary commissioned papers through four main approaches; (i) the school curriculum; (ii) teacher training; (iii) teaching materials; (iv) strategies. The main conclusions and recommendations in each of these areas highlighted the following issues:

(i) *Curriculum*
- embracing a subject oriented and multi-disciplinary approach including not only history, civics, economics, languages but also music and art;
- designing appropriate approaches from kindergarten through all succeeding stages of development;
- giving attention to the European spirit as expressed in values such as peace, human rights, tolerance, freedom and solidarity;
- addressing specific European problems such as unemployment and pollution and exploring their resolution through co-operation;
- encompassing extra-curricular activities including exchanges of pupils and students, European clubs, involvement of parents and parental organisations, and European school days.

(ii) *Teacher training*
- introducing a basic course to familiarise teachers with Community institutions;
- developing a multi-national training scheme for European awareness co-ordinators;
- networking amongst teacher training institutions;
- promoting work experience in other Member States.

(iii) *Teaching and learning resources*
- publishing more textbooks written from a European viewpoint;
- developing materials jointly organised between organisations and institutions catering for pupils at different levels;

- improving access to information about Europe including a central data bank;
- encouraging greater awareness amongst publishers of the need to introduce a European dimension.

(iv) *Strategies*
- exchange programmes for teachers and pupils;
- European seminars in close co-operation with Council of Europe and related organisations;
- improved information networks to achieve greater coherence, quality and effectiveness of activities.

It is interesting to note that many of the suggestions arising from the conference report and its main conclusion that 'the Council Ministers of Education meeting within the Council should adopt a resolution promoting the European dimension' (C.E.V.N.O., 1987) have since been acted upon or are planned. This perhaps indicates that whilst progress has been slow, gains are nevertheless incremental and cumulative in their effects.

The Teaching about Europe in the primary school project

Very little, if any attention was paid at the Maastricht conference to the particular needs of primary school teachers and pupils. The overwhelming bias was towards secondary and higher education. This situation remains an outstanding and substantial weakness in European educational policy making. One of the very few multilateral initiatives that have received E.C. financial support in this sector is the project that I launched in two phases from 1980 when the original proposal was first written.

The project was distinctive in four main respects; by adopting a collaborative and multilateral approach, encouraging teacher based research, producing case studies for comparative critique, and focusing on problems and issues in teaching about Europe in the age range five to thirteen years.

The aims of the project were derived from the view that:

- developing a European dimension was not simply about determining content, but about process too;
- talk of co-operation required a method that promoted agreements in judgements;
- practitioners needed to be enabled to play their part in clarifying policy and practice in a systematic way.

The project arose from a programme of European co-operation which began in 1977. From this initial work, a Network of European Teacher Educators was founded to promote joint programmes of study and professional exchange amongst its members (Bell and Pennington, 1981).

The project envisaged a collaborative venture between schools and teacher training institutions drawing upon the advice of members of the original network. The main aim was to establish 'action research units' to produce case studies of problems and issues in teaching about Europe in the primary school. The proposal outlined a pilot project in six Member States and made the assumption that during each year of operation two action research units would be established in different countries. Each unit would produce a case study of its work and make this available over an agreed period, normally twelve months. The project was organised by myself as project director from a co-ordinating teacher training institution. Action research units in Member States acted independently but were based in a sponsoring institution able to provide support for individual teacher researchers in schools.

A formal agreement described the various responsibilities of the project director, action research unit co-ordinators, individual teacher researchers, and inspectors, advisers and teacher groups. The agreement also outlined a calendar for achieving the aims of these units and set out details of the budget and how this was to be allocated.

The philosophy which underpinned this framework for European co-operation in educational affairs was based on a belief in the value of systematic investigations of practical problems of concern to prac- titioners as distinct from theoreticians; the benefits arising from linking institutions and agencies in different parts of an education system; the value of evidence supplied by teachers arising from the actual circumstances of particular schools and classrooms; and the worthwhileness of attempting to build up a body of practical knowledge which could provide a resource for future action programmes.

In short, the project was founded on the idea that what counted as 'Teaching about Europe' was best described by promoting action in schools and enquiry amongst teachers and that the way to organise this was to undertake action research on the problems and issues which the school and its community actually faced. Moreover, through various forms of co-operative discussion in which pupils, teachers, parents, teacher educators, advisers and inspectors took part, an understanding of relevant issues was expected to emerge. By recording this experience in a particular type of case study, practical knowledge, of use to practitioners and policy makers, would be made available.

The concept of action research refers to a method, developed by Kurt Lewin in the U.S.A. during the 1940s to systematically investigate practical problems. This method has been applied to a variety of settings including community relations, organisation development, and in recent years in the U.K. to teacher training. The main characteristics are that it:

- investigates everyday problems experienced by teachers;
- deepens teachers' understanding (diagnosis) of their problems;
- provides easily understood explanations;
- generates evidence validated by dialogue between participants;
- requires an ethical framework for the collection, use and release of data (Elliott, 1978).

The project action research units were established with a view to incorporating these characteristics. The choice of this method for a European project was that it emphasised the interests of practitioners, encouraged co-operation between different agencies and individuals, and promoted a framework of discussion to enable the study of similarities and differences in educational policy and practice (Bell, 1989a, b).

In these ways action research aimed both to assist in general problem solving and contribute to an understanding of specific practical issues in Teaching about Europe. Through requiring teachers and others to pose questions as to what ought to be done and testing possible answers by taking action on them, it necessarily required the involvement of individuals in planning and evaluating classroom practice. In this context of systematic investigation, action researchers found guidance in decision making. As a result this method was itself a learning process demanding both commitment to reflection and to action. On account of these features it aimed to enhance the skills of those who took part. Moreover, because it was to be conducted on both an individual and a group basis it had a propensity to promote a harmonisation of interests. This comes about through the political knowledge which necessarily arises in attempting to understand the practical details of another person's affairs. For all these reasons it appeared to be a particularly valuable method in a situation where international co-operation was a major aim. The cyclical form of action research is shown in figure 1.1 (below).

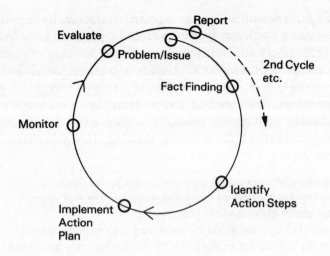

Figure 1.1 Action research cycles

Ten action research units in six Member States (Italy, West Germany, The Netherlands, Belgium, France and the United Kingdom) were established between 1982 and 1987. From the base of four people who met through the E.C. study visit scheme, the project came to involve an estimated 150 teachers, 30 teacher trainers and 40 schools.

The general conclusions were that this method worked well, was highly valued by participants at all levels and that such co-operation would probably not have been possible by any other means given the limited resources available. These outcomes suggest success in terms of communication, interaction and professional growth while the resulting case studies provide evidence for practitioners and policy makers alike.[8]

The following chapter examines in detail some issues identified through these case studies and draws out some lessons to be learned from the evaluated experience of the teachers who took part and the agencies who supported them.[9]

CHAPTER 2

Problems, Issues and Opportunities in Teaching about Europe

The Teaching about Europe in the primary school project was essentially a small scale action research project with a part-time staff and with funding which was subject to annual review. It was therefore a limited initiative that greatly depended on voluntary effort and goodwill.

In this chapter, I shall try to trace the ways in which the project operated.[1] My intention is to select some key issues which will hopefully illustrate aspects of organising multilateral projects and represent the experience of those who took part. The account is structured in the chronological order of the action research units which were established in successive years (see figure 2.1 below).

Aspects of project design and delivery

One of the biggest obstacles action research unit co-ordinators encountered in the project was the gap experienced between increasing recognition by some politicians and policy makers of the importance of Europe, and the perceptions of teachers, pupils and the public at large. This was a particular problem in the U.K. where due to traditional British insularity, the European dimension in the curriculum was, and still is, underdeveloped. But in other Member States there were very few specialists and schools were reliant on individual teacher interest and leadership. Among such teachers, there was the view that children in general were unaware of interdependent connections between Member States and knew little about the workings of

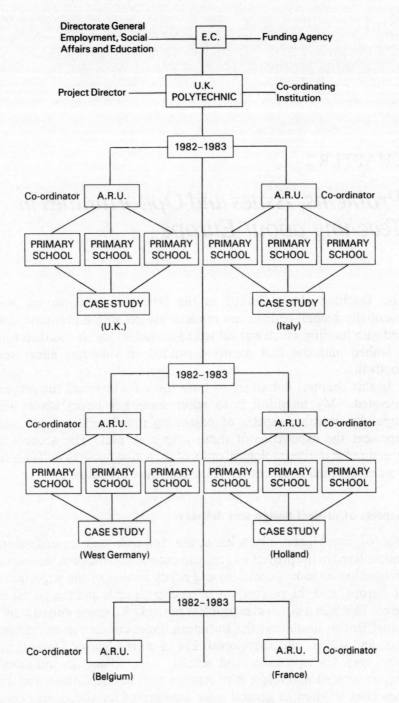

Figure 2.1 Organisation of the Project (subject to annual review)

the Community. Moreover, in many cases, adult awareness of Europe was considered to be even less well developed.

Resolving problems of Teaching about Europe should not be considered to be restricted to primary schools alone. Success depends in a large measure upon significant shifts in professional attitudes and public opinion. Action research projects, precisely because their methods of approach do require changes of attitude, knowledge and belief, are well placed to meet this challenge. For example, a significant question arising through the project experience was 'Which Europe are we talking about?'. Several units were concerned not to limit the concept of Europe to the E.C. As project director, I had quite deliberately not provided a definition of Europe. This decision was taken not solely on the grounds that this may politicise an otherwise educational project, but that such definitions in the context of collaborative action research must properly rest with participants themselves. The problem of definition was tackled in one West German unit by 'Europe' being thought of as a 'multiple living space' for millions (travel, work, economics, food), as a 'political region which has taken on a peaceful development' (borders, communications, twinning), a 'cultural region with a common history and traditions', and a many faceted 'ecological region'. These inter-related elements were seen to provide a conceptual framework for teaching purposes.

Another curriculum organisation issue was whether to take a 'permeation' model whereby the whole curriculum would be taught with reference to teacher/pupils awareness of the European context, or else to focus on specific subject areas, e.g. geography, history, economics, political and social (civics) education. Whatever approach was adopted, problems of *ad hoc* treatment of topics were posed leading to the possibility of superficiality, poor learning structure, reinforcement of national and social stereotypes, little in-depth preparation, poor participation by low achievers, undefined goals and underdeveloped evaluation procedures.

Rigorous clarification of the pedagogic value of a thematic approach was an implied challenge to practitioners of the 'Teaching about Europe' project if this was to be an educationally worthwhile experience for pupils. The project indicated that in-service training was necessary in schools where topic centred teaching was either not normally carried out or was poorly organised.

More specifically, the theme of Europe was not always mentioned in official curriculum guidelines and this was seen by some teachers and trainers to present a barrier. Vague general instructions in which teachers are asked to broaden their consideration of social and cultural events to a supra-national context appear to be insufficient to identify Europe as a topic relevant to primary schools. Bearing in mind that affective and attitudinal development largely takes place in pupils aged eight to eleven years, this situation, 'official' perhaps more by default than design, seems to be seriously flawed. What might be termed the 'default value' of the concept of Europe in the primary curriculum invites further analysis.

Current conceptions of multi-cultural education and anti-racist teaching in the U.K. can sometimes imply a restriction to curricula for pupils of Afro-Caribbean or Asian origin whilst in West Germany the same concepts would also include pupils of East European origin, e.g. children of 'guest workers' from Turkey. The alternative concept of World Studies is often taken to mean Third World Studies and be synonymous with Development Education, while the complementary notion of International Education is sometimes assumed to have the disadvantage of implying anti-nationalism. So it is that the more recent concept of inter-cultural pedagogy has been used to fulfil a role in overcoming the limitations of current educational terminology (Bell, 1987; Lynch, 1989). The possibility of a truly inter-cultural pedagogy arising from such debate will however depend on factors other than the trading of verbal tokens. Not least is the fact that educational frontiers are frequently defined by people who are not practitioners themselves which explains, partly, why there is no inter-cultural pedagogy despite a multitude of terms and definitions.

An effective knowledge base will not arise by supplanting one stipu-lative definition by a more prescriptive one supplied on higher authority. It will arise effectively at the level of promoting exchange of experience in a framework of communication which promotes the possibility of agreements in judgements and based upon the study of evidence. This is what the project attempted to achieve.

The rationale of this effort is based on the view that the main focus of current pedagogy, that of didactics (implying a science of teaching) is, at best, insufficient. It needs to be complemented by, if not replaced with, dialectics (implying skills of critical inquiry). Teachers in a modern democracy need to be, not merely technologists of information transfer, but facilitators of critique and dialogue, for only this will ensure active communication and interaction between teacher and pupil. In a modest and doubtless imperfect way, this situation is what the units were established to achieve. In order for such conditions to arise, certain barriers had to be overcome.

The first barrier arose from the fact that educational theory and practice has long been dominated by dependence on knowledge from recognised authorities e.g. academics, inspectors, professional researchers or politicians. Teachers have largely relied on such expert opinion. Moreover, even when placed in situations for which they have relevant skills they have typically exercised them in the context of training courses under the control of the same authorities.

Second, the institutional forms to which this type of educational knowledge has given rise has encouraged hierarchies in which truth is derived not so much from evidence but by deference to people in authority. Removed from the circumstances of practice, the interests of these institutions have necessarily been theoretical, supporting the pursuit of scholarship sometimes at the expense of practical insight.

Third, the dominant tradition of scholarship in European educational institutions has favoured the study of texts by individuals rather than collaborative practical studies. This has led to over-reliance on written evidence.

Fourth, even in practical studies, the use of scientific methods has prevailed. However, methods developed for studying causes in a material world are poorly suited to studying people and their values.

Fifth, the methods used in what currently counts as inter-cultural pedagogy have been influenced largely by the traditions of scholars of comparative education. In general, such studies have sought to reveal generalisations across cultures, or predict outcomes. This has led, as Stenhouse (1979) points out, to undervaluing case description and observation, and overvaluing theoretical and statistical evidence.

Finally, the development of pedagogy in terms of philosophy, psychology and sociology, has tended to result in all-inclusive 'grand theories', which are not supported by data and do not work because they are, at a popular level, incomprehensible. Glaser and Strauss (1967) distinguish this type of theory from 'grounded theory' in which descriptions and explanations are developed from data which are accessible to, and sometimes determined by, practitioners themselves.

The development of a knowledge base for inter-cultural pedagogy will depend upon the extent of progress in removing such barriers and their associated effects. In every case, the units established through the project were effective in modifying some or all of them. But, there is still much groundwork to be done in achieving conditions whereby the study of change is preferred to the study of texts; the collaborative investigation of practice is preferred to the experimental study of samples; and the focus of collaborative inquiry is on practical rather than theoretical issues.[2]

I do not suggest that these competing concerns are in other circumstances important, merely that for the construction of a practical professional knowledge base, certain pre-conditions are essential. Traditional pedagogy has effectively prevented the establishment of these pre-conditions and for as long as it persists, inter-cultural pedagogy will not develop effectively. On the other hand there are more immediate issues that act as constraints. For example one unit in Holland pointed out that Europe is considered a dangerous topic in the sense that not only do there exist a lot of opinions about it, there is also the requirement to transcend local and national cultures and this might imply giving a lesser priority to alternative regions of the world.

Europe may also be considered dangerous in a pedagogical sense for this topic means re-interpreting a long tradition of teaching which focuses upon the local as opposed to European environment. The major justification for this approach is that not only is the local environment more accessible for young children, it also provides a sound teaching strategy in moving from the concrete to the abstract. However, as the project demonstrated, one means of interpreting the local environment is to show how it is precisely multi-cultural. In this way, there is no necessary conflict with the prevailing theory of environmental studies teaching, even though in practice, perhaps, it may well have displayed distinct cultural or national bias. Such changes in the custom and practice of teaching implies a reduction in information along nationalistic lines. In the focused curriculum approach, the teaching of history (and 'civics' in certain Member States) may present less opportunity for fostering national identity and for some parents, teachers and politicians this may prove unacceptable.

In the 1987 Commission Report this factor is clearly recognised:

> Some educational systems are reluctant to enter this sensitive area which is subject to argument and dispute. Teaching staff are not always unanimous in the belief that the Community is a desirable necessity. It can only be approached via data which are examined objectively. (E.C., 1987:7–8)

One means of overcoming potential conflicts was perceived by some of the project co-ordinators, to lie in the direction of involving persons other than teachers in a teaching situation. While this can pose problems in certain Member States, the involvement of adults with wide ranging experience of relevant aspects of the European dimension in the curriculum was identified as a potential resource much under-used in schools.[3]

The particular contribution of parents was influential in several units and represents perhaps the single most important unforeseen positive factor in the project's experience. The impact on the multi-cultural setting of the classroom by both parents and in one case siblings assisting in demonstrating indigenous foods, songs, dance, traditions, costumes, and recalling events and illustrating ways of life, was substantial.

Other forms of co-operation, particularly in developing teaching materials, games and group activities jointly designed by teachers and pupils, brought a freshness and vitality often missing from commercial products. Moreover, the frequent unsuitability of published materials even when available, especially for younger children became apparent. The chief problems were cultural stereotypes, poorly matched text to age and ability, and no coherent theory of inter-cultural pedagogy evident in their design.

But, frequently, the teachers themselves, as sources of knowledge and information, were lacking either in personal experience or adequate training. For example, in the U.K. unit the project team felt vulnerable because of their limited awareness of possibilities. Meanwhile, a survey of 23 educational publishers carried out by the unit indicated there was perceived to be insufficient interest in the topic of Europe to justify the investment risk. This suggests that a vicious circle arises between the lack of good published materials, the low level of interest amongst primary school teachers and little encouragement for publishers to produce or revise resources for this sector of the market. Nevertheless, it was clear that the availability of good resources was an essential ingredient of success.

A most effective approach was found to lie in developing a portable data bank for teaching purposes which was school based and available on demand (Kasper *et al.*, 1990). Its structure was as follows.

Views across frontiers: resources for primary schools
Contents

1.	Slides	● Europe – a part of the world
		● People of Europe
		● Teaching situations
2.	Large photos	● Starting points for stimulating work
		● Notes on method
3.	Posters	● Flags
		● Money
		● Miscellaneous

4.	Games	● Travel games
		● Jigsaws
		● Dominoes
		● Search/placing games/card games
		● Games sheets
5.	Transparencies	● Skeleton maps
6.	Maps/globes	
7.	Reading materials/dances/songs	

Involving pupils proved possible across a wide age range from five to thirteen years. However, it was not always apparent whether the response of the children was due to interest in other (European) cultures or simply the open approach taken to learning and teaching.

The clearest evidence of self-motivated enthusiasm arose in the nine to twelve year-old band but there was limited opportunity to engage in active forms of international co-operation within the project. For example, the 1987 Commission report's suggestion of pupil exchanges and establishing a schools network 'linking one class or a number of classes to a common topic – so that teams of teachers are involved' (E.C., 1987: 18) would emphasise an empathetic dimension which only arises in circumstances where reciprocal relations are possible, but this has substantial implications for resourcing.[4]

Pupil involvement was crucially determined by the expertise evident amongst teaching teams in handling a topic centred approach. Similarly, the ability of teachers to adopt open learning methods reflected levels of prior training, availability of suitable resources, management experience and school climate. The U.K. units in particular indicated that pupils had very little first-hand experience of the European mainland and this was seen as a serious obstacle. The case study developed from the action research data put forward the following hypotheses for teacher researchers to explore further.

(1) Pupils do not normally see themselves as Europeans or recognise much relevance of Europe in their lives.

(2) Pupils regard Europe as an interesting subject for topic work because of the wide choice and flexibility of treatment which are possible.

(3) A pupil's vitality of interest in learning about Europe is closely related to the quality and amount of personal contact with things and people European.

(4) Pupils' opinions and beliefs about Europe are often simple and distorted but firmly formed and expressed.

(5) A programme of work closely restricted to written materials will not provide empathy with Europe or affect their attitudes.

(6) Pupils' attitudes and understanding are strongly influenced by productive contacts with visitors from Europe.

(7) Learning about Europe is an effective means of using skills of critical thinking to examine current affairs. (Ovens, 1985 in Bell *et al.*, 1989)

The teaching team involved in the U.K. unit concluded that 'Europe should be encouraged as a worthwhile component of the primary school curriculum contributing to environmental studies alongside work on the local environment and World Studies'. Similarly, one West German unit concluded that '[European] project weeks can be boosters or rewards but they must not be isolated or remain an exceptional event. Teachers and schools have to find space in their timetables and curriculum to continue the work.'

However, the Milan unit pointed out the need for fully involving pupils at different stages of development because 'for some children, the concept of Europe was too abstract. They sometimes perceive it but are never actually aware of it. Approaches and experiences for various levels must be devised.' Similarly, another unit in West Germany warns 'teaching about Europe requires great sensitivity to asking too much of children; there is the danger of over-taxing them through high demands and expectations.'

Project activities and products

Many interesting and ingenious activities for the children were developed by the teachers and support staff in the various units. A selection of these activities have been extracted from the case studies and are summarised in what follows.

Project activities in England (1982-4)

There were two units in England – Manchester and Sussex (Bell *et al.*, 1989).

As in the case of Amsterdam, the Manchester project was carried out in four schools, but whereas following the Dutch tradition, a 'whole school' approach was adopted in the Amsterdam schools with the headteacher usually being actively involved, the Manchester experiment was carried out by four teachers in their own schools in relative isolation from their colleagues, apart from one school where the headteacher also gave active support. In Sussex, neither teachers nor schools were directly involved in action research since none of those approached felt they could spare the time. The co-ordinator, therefore, carried out or observed lessons in two schools and conducted telephone interviews with eleven teachers in various parts of the country who were engaged in Teaching about Europe. The case study also contains a report of the work of a teacher in a Sussex primary school who regularly included a term's work on the E.C. in his geography syllabus.

In Manchester in school A, a class of 3rd year juniors (nine to ten years) took part. Several of the pupils had parents from Ireland, Italy, the Ukraine or Poland. For eight weeks in the second half of the Spring Term 1984, the whole class spent an afternoon a week on the project. They began with a general discussion after which the children chose a topic rather than a country to study. The teacher went round trying to help each child plan and carry out the topic. The emphasis was on finding out information and on basic mapwork to help children grasp the shape of Europe. A class display was organised with much of it being selected from materials brought in by the children. In addition, there was a class lesson each week on a different European country in turn, using maps and filmstrips.

In school B, a class of 4th year juniors (ten to eleven years) took part. A small number of children were from ethnic minorities. The aim was to develop a positive attitude to cultural differences. The general heading for the project was 'A Share in Europe'. Initially there were three blocks of three weeks duration each taken in sequence but because of a shortage of resources it was decided to teach the three topics simultaneously. This was done on two afternoons a week with an integrated subject approach. The teacher introduced the basic concepts. The children then worked independently or in groups guided by questionnaires. The themes for the three blocks were:

- 'Conflict and Co-operation': European events over the last 50 years.
- 'Common Interests': How European countries have worked together on specific projects.
- 'Ways of Living': Similarities and differences in life styles.

In school C, a class of thirty-four, eight to nine year-olds, took part. The teacher found the 'Other Children' series useful. She began by asking the children to write on the topic 'What I think about Europe'. This revealed considerable vagueness so they were asked 'What do they wish to find out?' The children produced a list of topics. These formed the basis of the project. About one fifth of school time was spent on this. The children usually began with a single country and then branched out to others. Use was made of visits to the class by mainland Europeans and the teacher ascribed changes in attitudes to these visits.

In school D, a group of ten, ten to eleven year-olds engaged in the project for a half day session a week. The children revealed considerable initial ignorance about Europe. Flexible use was made of the MacDonald 'Country' series of books and the children worked on themes such as 'food' and 'transport'. Work cards were used to direct their enquiry. Two of the teachers emphasised the important contribution made by carefully selected visitors. Commercially published games available at the time were thought to be of little educational value. One teacher recorded that simple concepts like 'county', 'country' and 'borders' were less well understood than she had expected and that teachers could easily fall into the trap of assuming that basic concepts were known by children when they were not.

In Sussex, the limitations imposed by the pupils' knowledge and awareness of Europe were explored by the co-ordinator in two primary schools during the Summer Term April–June 1983. The first of these schools was an independent residential school. The exploratory teaching sessions involved a voluntary evening activity once a week for ten to twelve year-old children. The composition of the group varied from week to week. The theme of Europe was explored from six different starting points. A seventh session was held with French children who were on an exchange visit to the school. These sessions are reported below.

- *Europe in the curriculum*. There was initial discussion of where Europe was likely to be found in the curriculum. French was suggested and geography also, but Europe did not figure in the school curriculum for the latter subject. The children suggested that Europe was 'just around' in films and T.V., especially news broadcasts, and to a lesser extent in newspapers. Some information has been acquired from personal contact and from family and friends. An essay was set on their impressions of a European country derived from a visit or a film. Physical features and food differences were described and there was an awareness of the language barrier. Although there were some chauvinistic comments, travelling to the European mainland had it seemed broadened the minds of some.
- *War*. Discussion followed a school debate 'That this house believes in nuclear disarmament'. The threat of nuclear war did not have as much impact as the Falklands War. There was some discussion of the First World War as some children had visited the battle areas. It was concluded that the reality of war was difficult for these children to comprehend and that benefits of peace were equally intangible.

- *France*. All but one of the children had visited France and there was an exchange with French school children. An assortment of French newspapers, magazines and children's books was circulated. As the children's grasp of French was inadequate these had to be translated for their benefit. They were able to identify similarities and differences. The French magazines were thought to put greater emphasis on clothes and food as opposed to the English interest in homes and gardens.
- *Politics*. A discussion was conducted about the U.K. general election and the European context. Some political personalities were well-known but there was very little detailed knowledge of public affairs and knowledge about political developments in other European countries was virtually non-existent.
- *Music*. A series of pieces of music from classical to pop were played. The children saw cultural differences in terms of different national experiences. There was very little understanding of a common European musical tradition.
- *The European environment*. A selection of slides illustrating landscapes, historical and cultural sites and scenes of everyday life from all the E.C. countries and one or two outside the Community were shown. The European countries were not seen as 'foreign' in the same sense as more distant countries with much more pronounced cultural, religious and climatic characteristics.
- *The school exchange link*. This was the first visit of the majority of the French school children to the U.K. Their knowledge of Britain proved to be at a very rudimentary level.

The second school explored by the Sussex co-ordinator was a voluntary aided junior school. The lessons observed were a formal part of the curriculum, with twenty pupils divided into roughly three equal groups meeting weekly on a rota system. There was an emphasis on core subjects in the curriculum with history and geography receiving less attention. The general approach was thematic topic work with an orientation towards local history and an emphasis on the development of skills. Questions were asked about a number of European countries but the children did not display a high level of European awareness and were largely ignorant of Eastern Europe. Some historical characters such as Marco Polo and Columbus were nevertheless recognised as Europeans.

The children were asked to prepare a short piece of written work on a character from French history. Most chose Napoleon Bonaparte but gave biographical information derived closely from their chosen sources and without any critical evaluation. All the group had visited Dieppe on a school outing and were able to describe architectural differences. French magazines were passed round and discussed and food differences were commented upon. It was clear that the children regarded France as a homogeneous unit and were not aware of regional cultural differences.

Concerning their knowledge of a European literary tradition, pupils were familiar with classical Greek and Roman stories but were not so well aware of Norse legends. They knew little of the historical origins of figures like King Arthur and his knights or of the European interest in such legends.

Teacher interviews

Of the interviews with eleven teachers who were known to be teaching about Europe in their schools in various parts of the U.K., four were based in Lancashire and had connections with the European unit attached to a teacher training college. These teachers had certain advantages when it came to resources and other help and carried out their European topics and projects on a larger scale than the other teachers surveyed. While there were obvious variations in content and approach, the typical teaching context of the remaining seven teachers was an integrated humanities approach beginning with the question 'What is Europe?'

After mapwork looking at the geographical aspects of the Community they went on to a country by country study of demography, topography, cities, currency, flags, codes, way of life and national characteristics of each member country. This was followed by a brief look at the historical background to Europe and the Community, 'How the Community started and why' and concluded with the Community today . . . how it works, what it does and how it affects the lives of people living in the Member States. Most teachers steered clear of Eastern Europe because of the political issues involved. Dealing with the functioning of the Community was considered to be by far the most demanding part of the European topic because 'the politics and policies of the Community are complicated and particularly difficult for the children to understand'.

It was felt that a topic based on the European Community was manageable if kept in simple terms. A productive approach was considered to arise from taking a specific issue confronting the Community and following it through. One teacher asked her M.E.P. to explain his work to the children. This he did with the aid of his diary for a typical week. Another started out from the working of the Parish Council and then developed her theme from Local Government to the U.K. Parliament and then the European Parliament.

Broadening the childrens' concepts of environment and community from the local to the global was an approach favoured by more than one teacher, as was encouraging children to see Europe in the local environment through looking round them and finding connections with Europe. First hand experience of holidays and travel abroad was found to be invaluable for the development of understanding.

The four Lancashire based teachers took a broader cultural look at Europe rather than focusing on the functioning of the Community. For example, the whole of one school simultaneously studied one European country (France) with the intention that spiral learning through successive year groups would result. Such an approach was also seen as compensation for the recent loss of French teaching in the school. Teachers put together their own data banks to assist teaching and learning activities and children were encouraged to bring in their own 'real' resources for example souvenirs, postcards, travel literature, food labels, etc. Parents, especially those who had lived in mainland Europe, also sent in materials.

Overall the teachers obviously felt themselves beleaguered through teaching an 'unfashionable' topic in a situation where humanities teaching in general and an integrated studies approach in particular were increasingly perceived to be under attack. They felt a sharper focus could have been achieved if there had been agreement on what 'about Europe' and 'the European dimension' meant. In-service training in European education was seen to be needed.

One Sussex teacher had devoted one term a year over the previous four years to work on the E.C. as an aspect of his geography course which was a part of a humanities curriculum approach shared with history. This course was taught with fourth year middle school children aged eleven to twelve. The work was planned and structured round Max Davies' book 'Europe Around Us' (Holmes McDougal) and was supplemented by information from newspapers, T.V., etc. He also found Moser and Ferrington's 'Europe Maps and Mapwork' (MacMillan Education) useful. The progression of topics was:

- Introduction: the idea of a united Europe – a short history of European development from the Romans to the Treaty of Rome.
- Europe – definition.
- East–West: The E.C.; the Eastern bloc; a division of ideas about how we live.
- Topography and demography.
- Population and topographical features, country by country.

- Trade – currency; imports/exports; tariffs; resources; communications; the Rhine. (Involving research in the local library.)
- Travel – children's holidays; the free migration of labour.
- Politics – ideas: culture, language, customs; political and administrative aspects of the E.C.

The experience of this course indicated that details of decision-making and implementation were the most difficult part for the majority of the children to grasp. These issues were studied in relation to the stages of settling a particular dispute. The approach was fairly formal. Comprehension exercises were set with carefully structured questions on the text. Mapwork exercises were also set. The written work was complemented by class discussion and the children were encouraged to organise their own work. It was felt to be important that this theme should be clearly related to the development of educational skills such as reading, writing, drawing, comprehension, interpretation etc. The children were enthusiastic and parental attitudes supportive. The children brought in food wrappers, labels etc. which were pinned on a board labelled 'We're part of Europe'.

Overall there was the universal cry that there was a lack of adequate and suitable materials. The teachers often felt under pressure to achieve too much in too little time. The children were easily confused by a diversity of topics and as a result all too readily lost sight of the underlying themes of unity and co-operation.

Project activities in Italy (1982–4)

Action research was carried out in four groups of schools in the Milan region co-ordinated from the Department of Pedagogy, Catholic University, Milan (Scurati, 1989).

Group 1 – Saronno: an industrial town 30km from Milan
The project was in a school with about twenty teachers. Five teachers took part, one of them as an external observer. The school headteacher co-ordinated the work and an educational psychologist acted as external supporter. The research took place over three months for a few hours a week. The general aim of all the class teachers was, 'The modification of an individualistic point of view in order to encourage a concept of European mankind'.

In class A, ten to eleven year-olds took part. The approach here was mainly geographical concerned with the interaction between mankind and the environment. It started out from work previously done on

Saronno as an industrial town. After a review of basic geographical concepts, classwork followed a scheme which was designed to help the children to work out how Saronno had developed with industrial, urban and technological development increasing and agriculture declining. The local reality was then compared to similar Italian and European developments. To some extent, the syllabus was constrained by the requirements of the traditional fourth form curriculum.

Class B also consisted of ten to eleven year-olds. As it was clear that a number of children from other countries and regions in the class were not fully integrated and not stimulated by their home background, it was decided to study the question of prejudice. A sociogram confirmed the isolation of some children. These were mainly children from Southern Italy whose parents had moved north in search of work. The children drew up a questionnaire to find out why individuals or groups of people migrate and administered it to the parents of pupils in a cross-section of classes in the school. A second problem arose spontaneously and was in turn investigated: 'What difficulties do emigrants find in their new environment?' Interviews and questionnaires were again used and photos were taken of graffiti directed at southerners. It was concluded that much discrimination exists against them. Parents also reported some similar attitudes by Germans against Italians generally. A further sociogram demonstrated that it was not only southerners who were isolated in the class and reasons for prejudice against individuals were discussed. The teacher recognised that these were sensitive issues but she had full approval and co-operation from all the parents involved. She felt that her own attitudes towards the pupils had improved and had resulted in their own greater involvement in class activity.

In class C, twelve to thirteen year-olds took part, combining two existing classes for this project. Both teachers were faced with the problem of how to introduce a European dimension into a traditional geography syllabus, and how to activate pupil directed problem-solving enquiry where pupils were used to traditional methods. Initially they had to introduce appropriate techniques. The teachers explained what they proposed to parents in order to enlist their support. Sixteen slides of European cities were shown to illustrate their proximity to seas, lakes, rivers etc., and in class discussion, a table was drawn up of common features. This was then extended to a further 50 European cities and led to a consideration of why plains, rivers and seas favour town settlements. The class looked then for other factors which had affected European settlements. These were checked in turn by thematic maps. It was said that 'The children shared a great deal of enthusiasm for the subject of the project'. The teachers judged that the pupils' participation in the study led to cultural enrichment and a greater understanding of the larger European community which went beyond the mere acquisition of superficial knowledge. Another teacher adopted a similar topic and strategy progressing afterwards to a study of distinctive cultural features. The children were able to describe characteristic aspects of English, Scandinavian, French and Dutch life. In the unit, all the children contributed to a study of folklore in Britanny. Written tests showed that the children had developed a good knowledge and understanding of European hydrography, climate, transport and economy. 'Moreover, by the end of the activity, pupils actually felt that they belonged to Europe. All the pupils participated enthusiastically in the first European School Day celebrations.'

All four teachers testified to the value of audio-visual aids, recording, discussions with external observers, and keeping diaries in improving their own professional approach and to the increased involvement and responsibility for their own learning shown by pupils. The support of the headteacher was an important factor in ensuring the success of an action research approach.

Group 2 – Milan–Gerenzano–Brusuglio

The group consisted of five teachers in the different schools. They drew their ideas from the regional in-service centre booklet 'Europe in the School'. The work of three teachers is summarised below.

In school A, in Milan, nine to ten year-olds took part. The teacher took as his topic two aspects of European culture: folk dances and houses. The aims were to pick out similarities and differences, and to involve parents. At a meeting of parents, two offered to supply recordings of music and visual materials. The research lasted four weeks. The teacher began by asking the pupils to complete a questionnaire so that he could find out what they knew about Europe and which would provide a base line from which the topic could develop. Most of the 19 children had some knowledge of geographical and cultural aspects and contact with people from countries other than Italy.

The pupils were provided with magazines and were asked to pick out similarities and differences. The pupils suggested a way of classifying these. Although they were all born in Milan, their parents came from different parts of Italy and their own and their parents' experiences

played an important part in their perceptions. Dances were then introduced since it was considered that music and dance were a universal
means of communication. They danced to the music and the
classroom discussion was recorded. The children obviously enjoyed
the experience and the teacher felt they had increased their empathy
with other cultural groups.

In school B, in Milan, twelve to thirteen year-olds took part.
Different aspects of Europe were discussed in a series of preparatory
lessons leading up to a consideration of the division of Europe into two
opposing coalitions each with its own nuclear arsenal. The focus for
this theme was a newspaper article. The topic concluded with a
discussion of a united Europe using a number of inter-disciplinary
approaches and utilising some of the material produced by the
European Commission. The teacher obviously found the content too
much for the time available and too abstract for the pupils to be
actively involved. She also felt threatened by the presence of external
observers and expressed a sense of isolation in her endeavours.

In school C, in Brusuglio, twelve to thirteen year-olds took part.
The topic here was 'food in the E.C. countries'. Again there was preparatory work in geographical and economic aspects of Europe and on
the functions of the E.C. The topic had four main aims; pupils should
experience the typical eating habits and diet of different European
peoples; pupils should know about the animal/vegetable sources of
such diets; they should understand the relationship of these diets to
geographical and historical factors; and they should understand the
main features of a healthy diet. The activity was based as far as
possible on the actual experiences of the pupils. At school they had a
typical English breakfast and then a German snack. Parents and
school staff helped to prepare this food.

Group 3 – Mede Lomelina: a small agricultural/manufacturing town
30km from Milan

Four teachers participated: three as class teachers and one as an
external observer. The general aims were to introduce the study of
Europe into the primary school chiefly as a means of developing
personal capacities and attitudes and to teach by encouraging
discovery learning and direct experience and enquiry.

School A consisted of eight to nine year-olds. The topic introduced
was an enquiry into local culture through looking at games related to
ways in which people spent their leisure time in different localities.
Pupils then proceeded to study jobs and diet, all in the context of the

past and present. Parents and grandparents were involved in answering questionnaires. Pupils followed up their own lines of enquiry, working individually, in small groups or as a class. A preliminary effort was made to investigate the pupils' own knowledge and attitudes as a base-line for development. Observations were made of the pupils' learning and it was considered that they had greatly benefited from the exercise. From an increased awareness of their own culture, they went on to a comparison with other European cultures. The help of an external observer was thought to be particularly useful. This very experienced teacher felt the whole exercise had brought about an improvement in attitude and techniques. She felt, however, that there were problems in finding curriculum time and space in a traditional school for such initiatives.

In school B, two twelve to thirteen year-old classes took part. The theme chosen by these two teachers was 'prejudice and tolerance' as a follow-up to work done on local culture (in the third form) and education about peace (in the fourth form). The project started with a sociogram which identified the degree of isolation or involvement of individual children within the class in the context of games or work. From this, the study radiated outwards to consider individuals or groups who were discriminated against in society. People with a variety of backgrounds were interviewed by the children about their cultural inheritance and experiences and this data gave rise to discussions and debates which were recorded and analysed. Through questionnaires and interviews at the beginning and end of the project, the acquisition of factual knowledge and the attainment of attitudes and cultural values were evaluated.

Group 4 – Gambolo-Vigevano: a large industrial town 40km from Milan

Five teachers agreed to participate. An unusual feature was that classes were small (5 to 15 pupils) and three classes included children with special needs. The teachers, who were less experienced than the Mede group, worked together and produced a joint report. They started off with a study of aspects of local culture as a prelude to comparative work on European cultures. As the project developed they became less interested in content and more interested in trying out a new way of working as a team in the framework of action research. For motivation to be sustained it was thought necessary that pupils' interests and experience should be ascertained and exploited. Information gathering was, therefore, closely linked to the pupils' surroundings. They formulated the questions for interviews and questionnaires which they then administered to parents and elderly people. Visits were made to a farmstead and a rice factory and this gave rise to a discussion of different work patterns, ancient and modern tools and leisure activities.

Project activities in West Germany (1983-5)

Schwäbish-Gmünd action research unit (Grass et al., 1990)
Nine class teachers co-operated with teacher training college staff to teach 24 lessons in seven schools. The policy was that these lessons should be self-contained units so that other teachers who might wish to try out similar lessons in their own school would feel free to adapt individual units to their own needs and should not feel constrained by the need to teach the lessons as part of a predetermined sequence. Nevertheless the lessons were seen as deriving from four broad aspects of the European concept:

● Europe as a multi-faceted living space for millions (units 1 to 8).
● Europe as a political region which must take on peaceful development (units 9, 10a, 10b, 11b, and 12 to 16).
● Europe as a cultural region with history and traditions (units 17, 18a, 18b, 19).
● Europe as a multiple ecological region (units 20 and 21).

It should be noted that the numbering of the units does not correspond to the chronological sequence in which they were taught though several teachers did start off with units 1 to 5. These were designed to introduce the idea of Europe as a multi-faceted living space and to ascertain what children already knew about it.

Fourteen lessons were taught in the audio-visual centre of the supporting teacher training college so that they could be recorded there. Children were bussed in and this added to the novelty and enjoyment. Reports were compiled by the training college staff and these are summarised below.

Bettringen school (nine to ten year-olds)
The children had already completed a topic about the Post Office in environmental studies. The teacher introduced the topic by describing the difficulty she had experienced in telephoning her home from another country. She encouraged the children to draw upon their own experiences of how things were different in other countries. Slides of Great Britain were shown and children were asked to write down the

differences they perceived. The teacher was surprised at their hesitancy in writing down peculiarities. She wondered whether the children did not have enough experience of other countries or whether tourists are to some extent isolated from experiencing differences in the countries they visit. Descriptions in the areas of food were more concrete. Pupils from other countries or regions showed more understanding than their classmates and provided vivid descriptions. The teacher decided to continue with this approach and to involve the parents of these pupils. The motivation and status of such pupils were judged to have been increased by the activity.

Kloster 1 School (seven to eight and ten to eleven year-olds: unit 18)
In the second year class there were six Turkish children out of a class total of 15 and in the fourth year class, two out of 20 pupils. It was decided to use the occasion of a major Islamic festival to organise a celebration in the two classes. The main responsibility was that of the two Turkish pupils in Class 4 but all the children took part in the organisation. The objective was to initiate an understanding of and respect for the religious beliefs of the Turkish pupils and people and to do a 'little towards raising awareness which would last a lifetime'. Turkish parents were asked to help and Turkish guests were invited as 'experts' to explain the customs and rituals. The idea was that this should be an experience to be savoured through all the senses, rather than an exercise to be evaluated afterwards. The room was decorated in the Islamic style with pictures, small rugs and other objects. While a traditional Turkish dish was being prepared, the children sang and danced. A Turkish carpenter took time off work to play and explain his musical instrument. The meal was then eaten, after which children and adults formed a circle and sang and danced together. The German children were surprised how much they enjoyed the meal and the teacher suggested this was because they had shared in its preparation. A German mother commented afterwards, 'In my view, we cannot do enough of these lessons. Only then will children behave in a way different to us adults'. The report concludes by saying 'Festivals could help to transform the school into a living space which is characterised by co-operation and an understanding of different points of view'.

Lorch School (ten to eleven year-olds: units 19, 1 and 12)
This class of 24 pupils included two Greeks, one Italian, three Yugoslavs and a Turkish girl. It was decided that the ongoing Christmas preparations should not be limited to Christmas in

Germany but should include customs in other countries. The children of migrant workers were given the opportunity to explain how Christmas was celebrated in their own countries. This enabled children to recognise common traditions and religious roots while realising that different feasts are celebrated or the same ones are expressed in a different way in other cultures.

Two months later, lessons were designed to find out how much children knew about Europe and whether Europe was a suitable topic for study. In the first stage, the children talked about what the term 'Europe' meant to them. They then drew a map of Europe and explained it. Afterwards they chose a European country to talk about and located it on the map. Their travel experiences strongly influenced their concepts, especially in the case of children from other countries. Their idea of the spatial relationships between different countries was very vague. Twelve countries had been visited by the children and their knowledge was mainly derived from these holiday experiences though they also knew something about imported goods, currency and famous sites. It was suggested that the maps used should be political with a minimum of detail.

The teacher reported that the exercise did stimulate an interest in the children to the extent that they brought material about European countries into the classroom. The amount of travel previously experienced by pupils was a key factor. The majority of children came from prosperous home backgrounds and this had obviously influenced the preliminary work. But it was considered that children from poorer backgrounds might be disadvantaged when it came to displaying their experience of other countries. It was felt desirable to go beyond the level of oral work. Certain concepts emerged more forcefully through drawing or role play.

The idea arose of producing a class magazine and daily paper and as a result, in unit 12, the class decided to focus on a particular issue which would introduce the class to the twin town of Oria. A representative of the town of Lorch had visited Oria and he came to give a talk to the class and show some slides. A delegation from Oria visited Lorch and the Mayor and his family came to talk to the children. He and his wife were both primary school teachers and so it was suggested that the children should make contact with their opposite numbers in classes in Oria primary schools and that the class magazine should be sent there. This was done before the summer holiday but would have to be carried on with other children, subsequently, as the present class would be moving on elsewhere after the holiday. The children asked a lot of questions of the visitors and interest was sustained over a long period. The report suggests that primary schools should be more generally included when twinning arrangements are made with other towns.

Linbach School (nine to ten year-olds: units 3 and 20)
Here, an attempt was made to see how far the children's concept of Europe was influenced by television and travel. The teacher asked the children to write down the ideas and thoughts which sprang to mind when given the stimulus word 'Europe'. The majority of the children wrote down the things in their local environment which might also be found in the rest of Europe. Only a minority named countries, important cities and sites and wrote down impressions of distinctive features of other countries. In retrospect, it was considered that the term 'Europe' was too abstract and more would have been contributed if the stimulus had been 'countries of Europe'.

The second lesson of three hours was based on the interpretation of European weather reports. The lesson was highly structured with a variety of methods and teaching aids being used. It was considered that simpler maps and spaced lessons of shorter duration might have helped pupils with learning difficulties.

Rechberg School (ten to eleven year-olds: units 8, 17 and 15)
This class carried out activities based upon three units. In the first, advantage was taken of the fact that in early May a change takes place in the produce being offered for sale in the local market. Locally grown winter and spring produce is still on offer but imported produce which is not grown locally until the summer is beginning to appear. This mainly comes from E.C. countries. The time seemed right for an investigation into the countries of origin of the fruit and vegetables, how traders fix prices and how customers react to them. This activity fitted neatly into the Ministry curriculum guidelines and gave the opportunity for several different kinds of learning to take place. A starting point was the birthday of a pupil. He would like a strawberry cake. Are they available? The children suggested questions to ask and the teacher arranged them into a questionnaire which the children took out to the market on the following day. Responses were taped, and most children took notes. Finally, the children bought some Italian strawberries.

Through observation and interview, the children learned a good deal about countries of origin, transport routes, freshness, quality and price of local or imported produce. They also learnt how to gain information and hopefully how to cope with their shyness.

Results were recorded on a sheet and discussed with the rest of the class. In the middle of May, the children visited a museum to learn about the Romans and to understand that a highly civilised people inhabited their region in earlier times. In this way it was hoped they would realise that the Roman heritage forms one element of European culture and they would become aware of living links with the past. The children were asked by the guide to put on togas and with the help of displays, models and maps they gained insight into the way of life of Romans and Teutons.

On the journey back, the children decided to organise a Roman Day. In the school library and at home they looked for books to obtain a more precise picture of everyday Roman life. The day was prepared by students on school practice together with pupils. They dressed up and carried out activities which gave the opportunity for different learning skills e.g. a Roman trial (direct speech), calculating tiling for a Roman bath (surface area) and the influence of the Roman language on our present day vocabulary. Some children also constructed a Roman watchtower at home with simple materials such as matches.

At the end of the summer term, the teacher read a story by G. Pausewang called 'Away with the Frontiers'. This was about two kingdoms which lived peacefully without any frontiers between them. The two kings were deposed by the Chief Ministers who built impene-trable frontiers between the two countries and began to prepare for war. The peaceful life which existed previously was contrasted with the repressive regime which followed represented by police, prisons and xenophobia. Eventually the people rise up and restore the Kings. The teacher suggested the children should dramatise the story. This was eagerly accepted by them and they worked for several days, allocating parts, preparing props, etc. At the end of term festival the play was performed for parents and the public who reacted enthusiastically to the message of the play.

Uhland-Bettringen (two parallel seven to eight year-olds: units 13, 9, 10, 11 and 16)
Several of the lessons at this school were concerned with frontiers. The topic was introduced by showing the children a cartoon of a smuggler trying to take some cigars through customs. When he politely raised his hat, all the cigars fell out. The children wrote a piece explaining the situation. This led on to one of the classes having a lesson on 'What are

frontiers for'. They were shown six slides of scenes at the Franco-German frontier without commentary and were asked to discuss what they saw and what its significance was. They drew on their own experiences and participation was very animated. Differences between the countries were listed on the blackboard. Children were then asked to imagine they were visiting a friend in another country and wanted to take a present. Where would they choose to go and what would they take? Then the roles were reversed. 'Your friend is coming to visit you. What should she or he bring by way of a present?' Presents were identified as a symbol of friendship and the theme was therefore thought appropriate for lessons attempting to induce co-operation and international understanding. Some of the children spontaneously wanted to continue the topic so they were invited to write about and draw pictures of their experiences abroad. The teachers introduced the lessons by reading a short piece about Germans being 'foreigners' when they travel abroad. A number of short but revealing pieces were written by the children. These were typed out by the teacher, glued to the pictures and mounted on the classroom wall. As the teacher explained, travelling is easier now than it was formerly. One child had been to five countries, but another, who was the son of a farmer, explained that farmers' families could not take holidays away from home.

The teacher pointed out that there is some danger that this topic might lead to children boasting about how many countries they had visited and that such comparisons might lead to a breakdown of co-operation in the class.

Several children pointed out that they were able to play with other children abroad even though they did not understand the language. The teacher felt it would be a good idea to follow up their awareness of language differences by conducting a lesson on translating words for everyday objects into different languages. The immediate occasion for this lesson was when one child brought a book from home in a foreign language and the children struggled to translate it. In their free choice periods a group of children drew an everyday object and then surrounded the drawing with the word for it in different languages. They also arranged a display of labels in different languages and made up a card game using everyday words in four languages.

The Ministry syllabus in environmental studies included a section on 'Grandparents, parents and children' and the teacher suggested to her class that they should interview their grandparents about what life was like in their youth. Travel abroad arose from this work. For some, this was associated with war or with being refugees. Otherwise, compared with today's children, few had opportunities for travel abroad. Although there was no follow-up to this particular lesson, the teacher felt that experience of travelling to other countries and regions was a useful contribution to international understanding and a way of counteracting prejudice.

Waldstetten School (nine to ten and ten to eleven year-olds: units 4, 5, 6, 7, 14 and 21)

Two separate classes had lessons on Europe in this school taught by the same teacher. In April she carried out a fairly formal mapwork lesson to find out what children knew about Europe and the E.C. The lesson enabled them to consolidate existing knowledge. They were highly motivated feeling this was useful knowledge which could give them status with their school fellows. They also wanted to draw Europe with its countries, cities and rivers as homework.

In a third year class, a card game was produced by the children and they made a wooden European jigsaw. In the card game lesson, the children contributed distinctive features of European countries and these were listed by the teacher on the board. When she felt they had sufficient understanding, she asked them to draw one of these features. In the main, children drew upon their travel experiences. In group work, they then put together eight or more sets of drawings and considered aspects relating to the different countries on cards. Care was taken that these should not be too big for the children to handle. A snag was that children tended to produce stereotyped images and features. The teacher also felt in hindsight that it might have been better to concentrate on the same four aspects for each country and to modify the game so as to equalise chances as children with a good memory obviously had an advantage. In this way it was hoped that co-operation would be encouraged rather than rivalry in playing the game.

For the jigsaw, the children drew the political map of Europe on a piece of plywood one metre square, filled in names of countries, capitals and important rivers, coloured in the different countries and then cut them out with a saw. The pieces of the puzzle could then be placed on a sidetable so that children could play with them at odd moments when they were free. For the purposes of the video recording made at the college the lesson was organised in such a way that the children rotated in groups between the card games, the European puzzle and a commercially produced European game taking about 15 minutes for each.

A follow-up to these activities was a unit in which small groups of children were asked to draw the map of Europe from memory. The shapes of the countries were not immediately recognisable apart from Italy and the countries tended to be drawn in relative isolation from one another. The importance of mapwork in helping children to form a more accurate idea of spatial relationships was stressed, as was the way children's emotional reactions to a country through travel may change their perceptions of it. As part of a series of lessons on the 'Post Office' derived from the State curriculum guidelines, the teacher showed the children a slide of a postage stamp which had a bridge motif and asked what the symbolism of this motif was. They worked out that the bridge symbolises the links between countries. The children were then asked to design their own stamps and to explain the symbolic meaning they were intended to convey. The range of motifs was surprising and contained the whole spectrum of ideas equivalent to the adult concepts of co-operation, exchange and peace in Europe. It was suggested that other motifs could be designed for a European cup or flag etc.

The children also visited a museum which had a unique collection of fossils. In this way, the children were introduced to the geological history of their local environment. The expansion to European aspects was later made in the classroom.

Reutlingen action research unit (Kasper *et al.*, 1990)

At Reutlingen, the unit established a project team involving 26 primary teachers in five schools. The European Centre in Tübingen gave help with designing resources and teacher training students assisted in the classroom. Each school then carried out a pilot project week of twenty hours on average in the summer term.

One of the most important objectives of the project team was to find topics that would exemplify local problems under European aspects. The approaches which proved most popular with the children were exhibitions and fairs, and musical and aesthetic experiences. There were two levels of organisation; small option groups where the pupils could choose a topic and the teacher associated with it, and bigger groups such as a school assembly when the work of a small group might be of interest to the whole school.

Typically during the project week, the usual morning timetable was abandoned in favour of integrated projects before break and options afterwards in which parents also participated. The case study comments that 'the outward appearance of the schools became more European each day'. European corners, display tables and exhibitions developed in every classroom. Occasionally there were special European rooms and corridors and the whole school building was used as work and exhibition areas.

The primary school centre in the supporting teacher training college was used as a workshop where data were collected and activities co-ordinated. Emphasis was not so much upon the acquisition of information as upon 'encounters with persons, institutions and objects, e.g. visiting a French school, Italian ice cream and pizza parlours; making things such as meals, a European jigsaw and such activities as selling exotic fruit during break'.

The project members were particularly interested in devising an appropriate approach for the youngest children, i.e. those in years 1 and 2 (aged six to eight years). The children were highly interested in the topics and liked talking about concrete experiences and thoughts. A lot of preparation and skill was demanded from the teacher who said that 'It seemed important to try and influence the formation of emotional attitudes and social prejudice since children of that age are very susceptible to these developments'. The teachers recorded that they proved unexpectedly adept with maps and globes though it was difficult to assess what degree of spatial understanding was present.

Aisbach School, Tübingen

In class 1a, the children collected information on Europe and looked at everyday life in the Netherlands, Denmark and Finland to see if they could discern common elements. These countries were chosen because they were all to the north of Germany. Also, one child came from Finland. Denmark is a popular holiday resort, and many Dutch products are sold in Tübingen.

The teaching objectives were that the children should become acquainted with each country, its position, customs and national dishes and should make comparisons between the countries. They should talk about Europe, ask questions and experience languages and songs from other countries. To these ends, they made a polystyrene model of the Netherlands, consulted travel brochures and identified the name of the capital, car number plates, the flag and national dishes. They prepared and ate a national dish, read or recited songs and fairy tales and sang songs in the languages of the countries studied.

Hohenberg School, Rottenberg

In class 2a, eight out of the 23 pupils were from other countries representing four different nationalities in the class. One country selected from Greece, Turkey, Yugoslavia and Italy was dealt with in turn on each project day. The teacher enlisted the co-operation of parents who played a prominent part in the morning activities. The class looked at pictures and photos, listened to fairy tales and tried out games from specific countries. They sang, danced, cooked and ate with parents and siblings of the children whose country was being talked about. The aim was to get to know other cultures, to further mutual understanding and contribute to the integration of pupils from other countries into the class. The teacher thought expressive activities were the best approach and that cognitive objectives should be postponed until later. Pre-structured teaching material and overloading the children with too much information or confronting them with problems was avoided. Activities within other classes were run by parents and, on the last day, all the pupils came together.

A third group concentrated on the way of life of the Lapps in northern Finland. Here the approach was more cognitive through listening, reading and writing to learn how one particular way of life catered for fundamental human needs. The case study suggests that this type of focus means that children miss out on the variety of European cultures available.

Altingen-Ammerbach School, Tübingen

This school provided an example of work with older children in three classes carried out by one teacher of ten to eleven year-olds and two teachers of eleven to twelve year-olds at a combined primary and secondary school. All the teachers had taken part in projects before and worked in close co-operation. A pilot European project had been carried out in this school previously. Fifteen per cent of pupils in the school were of non-German origin. It was decided to concentrate on U.K., Sweden and Yugoslavia on account of the teachers and pupils experience of them. Some time before the project week children were asked to write down what came into their minds when they were thinking about these three countries and the ideas were used to select topics which would be of interest to them. The morning timetable was structured so that they began in large groups, then broke up into smaller groups according to the country they had elected to study, then back into large groups for an interview. These larger groups were also used to look at other European countries. In the option groups, assignment cards were used. These were graded according to the child's learning ability and interest and gave the children help in structuring the material, finding sources and indicating lines of enquiry. For Yugoslavia, they were asked to find out about eating habits, draw travel routes, consider the country as a holiday resort, study the life of the people (clothing, customs and habits), identify tourist attractions and construct a miniature dictionary of key terms. The children who chose U.K. were asked to locate the counties, draw a map and find relevant photos, draw town maps, find out about customs and everyday life and find out about the currency, sports and houses. The children studying Sweden drew travel routes and maps, found out about the Royal family and read stories about Stockholm as a capital city.

In addition to these assignment card activities, most schools encouraged singing, dancing and cooking activities. On one Saturday, there was a meeting of pupils, parents, siblings and friends for the final event of the project week which included songs, plays, dances and a display of the work carried out by the children. Afterwards, the visitors toured the classrooms and enjoyed food prepared for them on the previous day. The children were encouraged to hand in written comments on the week and three pupils were interviewed on videotape about their experiences. The case study lists additional activities in other schools which the co-ordinators felt deserving of special mention:

- exchanging letters with schools in other countries,
- discussing town twinnings,
- producing books on Europe,
- visiting the market and finding out where fruit and vegetables come from,
- selling exotic fruit during break,
- selling French bread and pizzas to other pupils,
- visiting a Turkish carpet shop,
- looking at Italian, Greek and Turkish shops and restaurants – locating these places on maps – producing European games, jigsaws, card games, etc.,
- visiting a French school – visit from a French school,
- visits of guests from other countries,
- parents of children from other countries talking about their original home country and its ways of life,
- cooking, dancing and singing with foreign children and their parents,
- a 'flea market' in 'French surroundings',
- European Olympic games,
- European fairs.

Project activities in Holland (1983–4)

Amsterdam (Letiche, 1990)
In this case study, the co-ordinator and his colleagues were primarily concerned with the interaction which took place between teachers in the context of action research. The reports from the four schools involved do not, therefore, tell us a great deal about the topics which were taught or their effect upon the pupils who were involved. The case study explores the issue of facilitating action research on the topic of 'Europe in the primary school', in the context of an award bearing course (the collaborating teachers were registered for a Masters degree at the University). It also examines important issues in the management of learning, especially topic work, as an essential pre-condition to successful teaching.

In all four schools in the area around Amsterdam, Teaching about Europe was undertaken within the context of Social Studies. Generally, this had been taught by teachers working in isolation from one another. The approach had been to impart information, mainly, geographical, in a fragmentary manner divorced from the pupils' actual experience, following a prescribed syllabus or course book and then to assess pupils' absorption of this information by written work at the end. An attempt was made to introduce an inter-disciplinary, team approach with a more active participation in their own learning by the pupils.

In school A, the teachers of combined classes 4/5 and 5/6 took part using a course 'Where pupils live' combined with a project on a European country. The children followed an independent line of enquiry. As there was a considerable range of ability within each class, this presented problems. Children also tended to follow up a particular aspect to the neglect of others. Teachers had to give a lot of time to individual guidance and develop skills which needed to be acquired. The children were well motivated and carried out interviews outside school time. Pairs of children produced a term paper which reflected their creative activity and experiences.

In school B, all the eight teachers including the headteacher were involved. A social skills approach was adopted in which the children would learn to recognise and analyse differences between persons, groups and nations. Lessons took three half hours a week for three weeks. A closely structured approach was taken involving a progression from the immediate school environment for the younger children to regional/national aspects and then to Europe. The general theme was 'How do people live, work and relax?' The aims were that children would learn how to locate and use information, see the links between culture and the environmental context and understand and reflect upon cultural differences.

School C was a small school with four classes who followed up European aspects in a social studies context in a similar way to that described above.

School D was a school for children with moderate learning difficulties. There were nine classes of 15 pupils each running from age six to fourteen years. There were specialist support teachers as well as the headteacher. 'Europe' was felt to be too abstract a concept for the three lower forms so they chose a theme e.g. 'The farm' and identified a European dimension through this topic. The middle forms, age nine to eleven, took as their topic 'Where people live'. The upper forms with 35 per cent of ethnic minority pupils looked at the Second World War as seen through the published diaries of Anne Frank, the Jewish girl in hiding during the Nazi occupation of Holland. Connections were made by the children between problems of prejudice and discrimination then and now. Two further topics were undertaken 'Travelling by train through Europe' and 'The derivation of well-known European place names'.

Utrecht action research unit (Galesloot and Ten Brinke, 1989)
The project was carried out in two schools. In P.J. school, work was spread over two months though there was a review at the halfway stage which resulted in a change in organisation. In the K.V. school, the project lasted one month.

In the P.J. school, two classes involving twelve to fourteen year-old pupils participated. In the beginning, a morning and an afternoon a week were used but it was later felt that shorter more frequent periods would be better and additional time was given at the end of the project for the preparation of a presentation. The main aim was to stress the growing interest in Europe. In history, prominent European figures of the past were studied together with past conflicts as the reasons for present-day co-operation. Geographical knowledge about the countries of the E.C. such as location, borders and important towns was acquired. Common ecological problems were explored.

A brainstorming session was held in which a list of European topics was compiled. Children were then free to choose which aspects to concentrate upon. They were asked to bring materials from home relating to these aspects. Control was exercised by the teachers issuing guidelines about working in groups and using resources. Children were required to complete a weekly record sheet of activities which was checked by the teacher. They produced folders of work which contained drawings and pictures, data and photographs of the country chosen. They also worked towards a common final presentation. This consisted mainly of a series of short dramatic episodes in which everything was designed by the children themselves and in which all the children were involved in turn. Nine countries were dealt with in rapid succession. The teachers commented that the children were more interested in preparing their own presentation than in listening to and learning from the others! This approach might, it was commented, result in the children not getting a sufficient grasp of the E.C., though the first phase may have been useful in arousing initial interest in Europe as a whole. A résumé of the countries and aspects portrayed in the final presentation is given below:

Holland	– maritime history and shipping, the Dutch flag,
Belgium	– cooking styles and beer production together with other more general information,
Luxembourg	– history, geography, languages and currency. Benelux – the coal and steel community,
U.K.	– the speech from the throne at the opening of parliament – the miners' strike,
West Germany	– holidays in Germany – costumes illustrated with dolls,
Greece	– a guided tour of Athens – language – a Greek folk dance performed,
France	– French cars and British car sales – French food – historic buildings – a fashion show is held,
Denmark	– a travel agency tells a tourist about things to see,
Italy	– one child provides continuity whilst the others deal with eg: greetings and currency, the history of Rome, the Vatican, Italian food, the shape of Italy on the map and historic places to visit.

In the K.V. school, classes combined on a whole school basis. The project was carried out on two afternoons a week for a month. The teacher introduced the project to a meeting of all the children by dressing up and greeting the children in the various languages of the community. They also showed slides of typical features and played music of the various countries. The children called out the name of the country and the teacher marked the location of the country with a flag on a display of the E.C. countries. Further slides were then shown. The children responded very positively to this innovation. Parents were also consulted through a letter which described the project. The teachers did not want to impose any initial framework on the activities of the children but to use their experience and interest as a starting point. In the twelve to thirteen year-old classes, the teachers asked 'What do you want to do about Europe?' and a list of the children's contributions was drawn up on the blackboard under various headings such as food, defence, language, etc. Each child was then asked to choose one or more aspects and advice was given about finding out information, method of working, asking questions of parents, etc.

A similar approach with children aged nine to eleven years produced suggestions about making flags, collecting things, making a travelogue and words in different languages. The first two classes of children aged six to eight years sat around in a circle and showed each other things brought from home from different countries.

In general, the children worked fairly independently but learnt to co-operate with one another in small groups. They were very busy and highly motivated because they felt they were following lines of enquiry that they had initiated themselves. The teachers acted as stimulators to learning activities.

The teachers of the twelve year-olds group felt that they had to be more directive when it came to the children acquiring information about the function and aims of the E.C. and the value of this form of international co-operation. The two teachers of the six to eight year-olds felt it was important that they had agreed the main lines of the development of the project towards helping children to appreciate that all countries are different. They were surprised at what the children already knew. As one of them said, 'I had not thought that the children, because of their age, would be so interested in this topic. They also know more than I thought'. This was endorsed by a colleague: 'The children appeared to know already a lot about travelling to foreign countries, borders, etc. They like to talk about it'. Nevertheless, they also reported that the project was a bit too long for these children to sustain interest and the periods spaced too far apart for them to maintain continuity. It was also a bad time of year because the teachers had not had sufficient time to get to know the children and the children were involved in other major projects connected with Autumn and Christmas.

By the end of the project, children had produced a variety of work. In the upper school, the stress was on written reports and booklets containing pictures and press cuttings about the E.C. In the lower school, the emphasis was more on drawings. In all the classes other things relating to Europe were produced such as passports. The teachers commented, 'The walls of the classroom were gradually filled up with items to do with the E.C. and with individual countries of the E.C.' In addition, each group in the upper school had made a survey of a country on a sheet of paper. The sheet contained a small map, a survey of coins, language, form of government, head of government, some important economic activities and typical products, the flag and some topographical data. The children enjoyed the project including the method of working. They wanted to know more about the E.C. and suggested that a special paper about the E.C. should be produced for children and schools. The main problems for teachers appeared to arise from the relatively unstructured approach. The teachers of the older pupils commented, 'I have a few problems with it; a very un-structured introduction is less suitable for this topic' and 'I must admit it is interesting to see how it develops, whether children left to their own devices will be fully occupied. The informal style of working is difficult for me: I lose track of what is happening'. Those from the nine to ten year-old classes thought that, 'Such a style of working is difficult. I have concentrated on the need for co-operation', and from the lower school, 'The children bring more things from home than can be dealt with or used'.

Teachers also had to prevent children wandering off on a side-track. Overall, they were satisfied that the children had acquired insight and learnt co-operation in looking up and processing information but were less convinced that they had acquired knowledge and insight into the functioning of the E.C. As one teacher of other pupils said, 'If you let children work freely in this kind of teaching they are mainly going to collect nice pictures, travel brochures, etc; the E.C. as a functioning body is not very alive'.

Project activities in Belgium (1985-7)

Mons action research unit (Koval-Gillard, 1990)
The project was carried out in a number of different institutions and with children of different age levels.

S.J. School - Angleur
The school was involved in a process of innovation in methods and curriculum towards making the approach more child-centred so that

there was already a ferment of new ideas and a willingness to adopt a European dimension. The project was mainly carried out by four teachers in the twelve to fourteen age group. An example is given in the case study of a typical school day. For part of the day, pupils took on individual written contracts, with the advice of the teachers, to carry out assignments in reading, mathematics and French and to tackle two workshops a day in the sciences, geography, history and drawing. Some ten activities were dealt with in this way in rotation. They worked from a guided questionnaire with a European emphasis. Follow-up work was also carried out at home. Practical work and the information which had been collected were presented to the whole class. The children were enthusiastic and learnt how to take responsibility for organising their own enquiries. Parents also were, on the whole, very helpful and the teachers noted a readiness to break out of the rather parochial outlook which had hitherto characterised the people of Liege. This perceived shift they attributed to the economic pressures of unemployment and inflation.

C.P. School – Baelen

In contrast to the previous school, the European project was not an official part of the curriculum but had to be brought in by the teacher as and when opportunity arose. He was responsible for second language (German) teaching in the upper forms and also for remedial work with small groups. In this work, he used games as a teaching aid and so decided to try to develop a European card game with groups in the fifth and sixth years. The children would not only collect information about European towns but would also work out the rules for playing the game. This would involve learning how to co-operate.

The teacher started off by finding out how much the children knew about the E.C. countries. This was disappointingly little and mainly derived from holidays abroad. Starting from German cities, they built up a card index of about 250 towns. The idea then arose of putting them in sets according to similarities and differences. To overcome the language difficulty it was decided to draw pictures, for instance, of famous people. Several different ways of playing the games were worked out. The teacher then got into touch with a firm producing playing cards and it was decided to produce 6 series of 52 cards, grouping certain countries together.

Some difficulties were reported of colleagues who apparently considered devising a card game was not a very worthwhile scholastic occupation! Nevertheless, the teacher felt it generated a number of useful learning activities from which these particular pupils profited greatly.

U.S.L. School – Mons

This school had nursery, primary and secondary pupils on the same campus. The general spirit was innovatory. All classes were taught about the European dimension though the project described in the case study was carried out with the age group of twelve to thirteen year-olds.

For several years, Europe had figured in the syllabus and the children regularly listened to news bulletins on the T.V. which included European news items. These raised questions which the pupils were encouraged to research in the library. The aim of the project was to study these points systematically and to include a study of the E.C. from a geographical point of view. The children were given a scheme under some seventeen headings embracing geographical and cultural aspects and were asked to find out information which illustrated characteristic features of the different countries. Information was also sought by the pupils from embassies and from the European parliament. Some delegates came to give a talk about the work of the E.C. The pupils were judged to have performed 'brilliantly' on a question and answer session on the E.C. A large display board was put in a prominent place in the school. This was divided into fourteen categories and pupils and their parents contributed items. The overall project was judged to have made a lasting impact.

F.P. School – Chapelle-lez-Herlaimont

There were four nursery and thirteen primary classes in each case on two sites. The occasion of a triennial children's festival was taken to organise a variety of activities with an E.C. focus. The whole educational community was involved pupils, teachers, management and parents. The preparation began several weeks beforehand with the nursery classes being responsible for displays associated with two European enterprises – the Ariane rocket and the European year of road safety. They made small model cars, built a rocket and dressed up as astronauts and launched a small rocket. A number of foodstalls provided the specialities of different countries and a number of side-shows were managed by the school children themselves. (Raising money for school funds was one of the objectives!) Classes performed dances in turn from different countries to appropriate music. Considerable research into the geography and cultural variety of the

Community had been carried out beforehand. The school authorities involved the local newspaper which reported that 'We can only applaud the events of this day and we take the opportunity to congratulate the teachers of the F.P. school of Chapelle.'

Nursery teacher training college

The project was envisaged as part of the practical school experience programme of 21 students in 19 schools. They taught classes of five year-olds for about two weeks. Students could opt out of the European experiment if they wished but none did so, although they – and the class teachers they worked with – were rather sceptical to begin with, partly through unfamiliarity with this approach, partly through lack of experience of the portfolio range of children's responses.

Many classes included immigrants and to some extent this influenced the choice of country to be studied as well as the familiarity of some students with particular countries. A general complaint was that students lacked adequate information although some attempt was made to remedy this in the initial preparation and also to acquaint them with conducting action research.

A very large number of lessons were prepared including handicrafts, number games, logical games, verbal games, posters, flags, drawings, models inspired by the rich cultural and artistic backgrounds the theme of Europe presented. Windmills, clogs, mouldings, double-deckers, the Eiffel Tower, gondolas, the Leaning Tower of Pisa, the Dome of Florence, Greek Temples, senoritas, castles, the Atomium, landscapes etc., were investigated or built individually or collectively. Culinary recipes were made, e.g. Brussels pâté, pizzas, kebabs. Folk music, dances and chorus songs were also part of the activities. Certain religious lessons presented the Pope and Lourdes.

The project also involved the 'twinning' of the classes with another school, visits to museums, community meals, and information and presentation of the project work to parents. The common objection made by some educationalists that one should not 'teach' in the nursery school was rejected by this particular group:

> we can assure you that to travel in a double-decker, paint a mural, put on a costume of somewhere else, dance to another kind of music, sing in another language, discover other places, go through Italy accompanied by Pinocchio, travel on an international train . . . even if this one is made of cardboard . . . may be only a beginning but it is a promising one.

The reactions of the class teachers were sounded out informally at their initial meeting with their students and more formally at the beginning and end of the experiment. Cautious approval was the fairly general end result but the teachers themselves were felt by the co-ordinator to be woefully undertrained when it came to the European dimension.

Similarly, questionnaires about their experience were given to the students. They felt that the choice of topic was a good one and the children had very much enjoyed the work. They were aware that they had often fallen short of what they set out to achieve. This lack of confidence was considered to be inevitable in students who are aware of being 'on trial' and afraid of failure in an area where they lacked information.

The College staff felt that if the experiment were to be repeated, there should be a more thorough preparation of the students and some class teachers should be involved in this to give them a good feeling of being partners in the project which would also be good for their own morale. The regional primary school inspector who was also a member of the assessment panel put forward a number of suggestions for improving the way the project was carried out. She suggested a longer period of slow, steady permeation in which the topic would be initiated by the student and continued by the class teacher in co-operation with other classes and ending with a school project. She thought the students had an approach which was too academic and that they should make their approach more human and personal. She considered that in this way mental portraits would be gradually built up of children in other countries. This approach would be strengthened by the school and parents organising an exhibition on 'Children as European Citizens'.

R.S. School
The project undertaken in this school formed part of oral and written work in French carried out by a teacher with a group of eight pupils who were all born in Belgium but whose parents had migrated from other parts of Europe. The work was carried out over four periods with twelve to thirteen year-olds.

In the first lesson they were asked: 'How do you conceive of Europe?' They had different perceptions according to family background. They were then asked: 'Where do you see Europe in the market?' Their observations came in different categories. In the next lesson they decided to draw two maps; one of the Europe of the twelve, and one of Africa to show the country of one of the pupils. A discussion of culinary differences arose from their observations in the market so it was decided they should each bring along a family recipe.

This work, which involved the use of dictionaries and atlases and a piece of writing, was carried over into the third period. In the fourth period they were shown an article in the local newspaper about the E.C. 'Europe grows to twelve/slowly' (a play on words in French) and were asked to comment on it. The idea was that they should critically examine the lay-out, the information and the way it was presented by the article.

Project activities in France (1985–7)

Nancy action research unit (Garcon and Prat, 1990)
The project was run as an in-service programme from a regional centre. The general theme was 'Teaching about Europe: teaching continuity in nursery, primary and secondary education'. The idea of continuity was introduced so that teachers in institutions which normally had different types of in-service training could be brought together in one programme. This was facilitated by the fact that the three schools were on the same campus and the organisation was in the hands of the headmaster of the secondary school who was also a member of the co-ordinating team.

A joint planning meeting for all seventeen teachers in the project took place and a brainstorming session resulted in a number of topics being suggested under five headings:

- environmental aspects of European countries,
- cultural aspects of European countries,
- E.C. organisation,
- European identity,
- children in Europe.

Planning of units then took place in two groups; teachers in nursery and primary classes 1 and 3, teachers in primary classes 4 and 5 and secondary classes 1 and 2. Teachers then taught the units for three months. They returned afterwards for joint evaluation meetings. A highlight of the project was the European Christmas party in which 250 children and a number of parents were involved.

The topics for the various classes are briefly described below:

Nursery school

Children two to four years old (two folders of work)
(1)   Wildlife and plants in Europe. Drawings, etc.
(2)   I am two, three, four years old. What does Europe mean to me? Photo-

graphs, texts and drawings about differences in songs, speech, animals, trees and flowers etc.

The children handled objects and developed skills in classifying and locating information, drawing and creative expression generally. They were judged to have developed self-confidence, co-operation and freedom of expression. The emotional environment similarly greatly improved.

Children four to five years old:
How European children spend their time in school.
A collective folder and some individual work.

The children were able to develop an idea of the sequence of days, counting and the sequence of numbers generally. The children were constructively involved in the work and parents helped out with information.

Children five to six years old:
Special days and customs in Europe.
One folder of work.

Feasts in various European countries were described and illustrated by the children with texts, drawings and photographs.

Primary school

Children seven to nine years old:
Putting together a file about 'Europe': a folder about special days and customs, with photographs, texts and drawings by the children.

The objectives were that children should be able to name the E.C. countries, locate them on a map, locate their capitals and compare their populations and topography. They should also develop skills in findings out and organising information.

Children nine to ten years old:
Using computers, they worked out a programme for drawing flags, and made use of software to present:
● consumption of some kinds of food in each E.C. country,
● consumption of one specific kind of food.

The pupils constructed data charts, histograms and pie charts for ten products from each E.C. country and for one product in all the E.C. countries. Through these activities skills were developed in reading a table of numbers, dealing with proportions, percentage and scales, and using information technology.

Secondary school

Portuguese. The children produced a bilingual book: 'A book, an age, a country' and undertook the marketing of the book themselves. With the proceeds, they hoped to organise a visit to Portugal. The teacher observed that such work as dramatisation, preparing an exhibition, making up a volume helped the children who took part to increase their sense of personal identity.

English 'A trip to Newcastle'. The children assembled information about the twin town of Newcastle and the twin school involved including everyday English life, English food, T.V., entertainments, people, streets and shopping. Besides the usual benefits derived from these twinning arrangements such as discovering a new country, new people, different ways of life and customs, increasing knowledge and becoming more open-minded, it was not the expected improvements in the standard of spoken and written English which was judged to be the chief gain. The teacher observed that general attitudes to school changed in a positive way. The pupils rediscovered motivation and intellectual curiosity, became eager to speak, to communicate and to learn and were less anxious about unfamiliar experiments.

Inter-disciplinary and inter-age level activities
An exhibition was mounted with 25 panels organised under different headings:

- history and institutions of the E.C.,
- Europe compared to other civilisations,
- European currencies,
- Portugal: its history, geography and culture,
- Europe: some regions and capitals: London, Paris, Milan,
- the London area,
- the North Sea,
- tourism in Mediterranean regions,
- tourism in the Alps,
- European culture and education,
- hygiene in Europe.

In the entrance hall a display board was erected 'Europe and the News'. It was regularly kept up to date by the pupils who contributed information about current European events. Collections of pupils work were produced for exhibition:

- 'Europe': myth or reality?
- work in mathematics,
- a trip to Strasbourg (photographs),
- the book on Portugal produced for sale.

Other displays included a rotating screen which showed the number of T.V. sets in each country of the E.C. per 1,000 inhabitants; some software about the E.C. countries and common symbols e.g. flags and national anthems. A video film 'France and Europe' from the regional in-service centre was supported by computer software about the E.C. tracing its history, geography, demographic and economic aspects. The software included a computer based questionnaire for pupils going to the exhibition to assess for themselves their knowledge of Europe.

Pointers to good practice from the project experience

If we now review each of the case studies in turn to consider some key issues arising, in England the case study suggests that, 'a major learning outcome had been the acquisition of a great deal of knowledge about Europe'. Skills had developed and there was firm agreement across the team that:

> Teaching about Europe not only provided excellent scope for the development of research and higher order reading skills but also that it had brought more success in this area than comparable project work based on a different theme. The main reason was the interest generated.

The team recorded 'the growth of critical thinking'. Most of the time, however, evidence of attitude change eluded direct attempts to collect it. Nevertheless, one of the teachers was able to record some examples which indicated that 'they were usually related either to some kind of personal contact with Europe or the discussion of current affairs'. Another 'found radical changes attributable to the European visitors to the classroom'. The main issue, the inclusion of Teaching about Europe in the primary curriculum, was viewed somewhat differently by different participants. However there was fairly general agreement at that time that Teaching about Europe gave adequate opportunities for:

- the expression of good primary practice,
- the development of reading and research skills and critical thinking,
- successful multi-disciplinary thematic/project work,
- the growth of European cultural awareness.

The case study also recommended that 'Europe should be encouraged as a worthwhile component of the primary school curriculum contributing to environmental studies alongside work on the local environment and World Studies'.

The Manchester unit concluded that 'For Teaching about Europe to take its place in the primary curriculum, strong support is needed at a high level to ensure the organisation of appropriate human and material resources'. This general finding was confirmed by the Sussex unit. Here it was accepted that in terms of generating action research the initial research phase of the Sussex enquiry had been a 'failed' experiment. At an early stage, 'it was acknowledged that there should have been a fuller more extensive effort to find sufficient resources and suitable contacts. The study suggests that 'it was unrealistic to expect teachers to jump at the proposal without adequate resources both financial and material and particularly when they are under considerable timetable pressures'. The co-ordinator concluded that 'the most productive strategy is through a European dimension approach; themes in history, geography, languages and environmental studies rather than trying to establish European Studies *per se*'.

In Milan many teachers were constrained by the need to teach within a fairly traditional subject-based curriculum. Their initial preoccupation therefore was with finding content with a European emphasis which would fit in with this curriculum. As the research progressed they became more concerned about the effectiveness of their own teaching methods. Teachers became highly motivated by what they felt was a productive method of action research to address this issue. They became more tolerant, confident and co-operative with colleagues and the use of new tools and evaluation techniques led to more efficient and creative teaching. They considered that:

> the introduction of the study of Europe and European education in the school curricula greatly improves the pupils' learning and active participation, that is, it leads to a better and more specific acquisition of concepts, a more pertinent ability to formulate questions and propose research projects, a more developed capacity to consider ideas and a greater open-mindedness.

As in other studies, 'the majority of teachers considered the concept of European education for the pupil to be as much about the development of personal skills and attitudes as the acquisition of specific subject-based knowledge'. The reactions of pupils were invariably positive; they showed greater commitment, confidence and participation, a 'group spirit', a 'new atmosphere' of disciplined participation arose. The increased use of audio-visual techniques similarly improved the quality of pupil–teacher interaction.

The case study acknowledged that the evaluation of changes in pupils' attitudes and behaviour with regard to empathetic objectives was particularly difficult and:

> what is achieved inside the school can only provide a partial answer to the question of whether the objective of acceptance of other cultures has been achieved. Teacher research was limited to the school and would have had to include an analysis of the effects of the family and the wider social environment to be meaningful in this regard.

At Schwäbisch-Gmünd, despite some tensions between the process of action research and the content of the project the project team felt there were positive gains. 'At least, we have made primary school children interested in Europe.' They also acknowledged they had opened up a new field of research for 'the emerging picture of Europe is open for further developments in future research projects. It has pointed out possibilities but one would have to approach it on a more modest scale under normal teaching conditions'.

One positive gain was judged to be that teaching about Europe integrated children from other countries more strongly into the class since 'it has partially changed the attitudes of the German children'. Another general finding was that children can expand their:

> knowledge about Europe if their experience forms the basis, if they are given the opportunity to express themselves and if the information is provided at their level or linked to practical activities. Modern theories of learning which state that only such knowledge as offers personal, subjective points of contact will become meaningful and significant have to be taken into account especially when Teaching about Europe in the primary school. Active participation has its limits and therefore pictorial and visual instruction, via texts, slides and films must be used in the absence of direct encounters.

The approach produced a high degree of motivation and interest in the children and the study concluded that 'the primary school children have expanded their knowledge of Europe. They have formed attitudes to other nations, boundaries, peace and understanding and they have started to be interested in Europe'. The report of a group of lecturers held in July 1985 summed these gains up:

> All project members see as a success that all teaching units initiated interest in Europe in teachers and pupils and that this interest became evident in further activities. Another success was that for those six months they managed to carry out a wide variety of methodologically different approaches to Europe. This was attributed to the chosen procedure which was considered productive.

The Reutlingen study congratulated:

> all who helped us make this project a success. The competent and self-assured attitude of the children during the final project meeting was impressive. The children did not seem to grow tired of these European activities. Whenever the children watching the final performance had a chance to show off their knowledge, they were proud and keen to do so.

The response of parents was particularly enthusiastic and appreciative and the Parent–Teacher Association of Baden-Wurttemberg awarded the project a financial prize in a competition 'Parents for Europe'. Exhibitions were mounted and courses were run to disseminate the results to a wider public. Efforts were made to make the materials and resources which had been produced more generally available to teachers but the exhaustion of project funds threatened to curtail the further exploitation of what had been achieved. It was noted that after the first exchange of experiences and the final exhibition of project work, contacts between teachers grew considerably fewer, probably because schools and pupils had to go back to other normal activities and their 'work potential declined'. As the case study points out, such intense activity could only be sustained over a relatively short period of time. The dilemma was how to convert these short periods of intense activity into a permanent influence on the curriculum.

In Amsterdam, the unit concentrated upon in-school transactions arising from the project and led to an initial diagnosis that 'while educational experimentation to strengthen social learning and conceptual integration is common, the resulting topic based approach shows (up to now) more pedagogic confusion than clarity'. This the researchers put down to the reluctance of teachers to submit to an examination of their own processes and to share their insights with others.

The Utrecht unit commented that the aims that the teachers in one of the two schools had for the lower forms, namely to create interest in Europe and to alert children to the fact that Holland was different from other countries, were achieved. The children were very enthusiastic and the teachers were satisfied. In the higher forms (at the same school), teachers were satisfied that the children had developed skills of deliberation and co-operation in looking up information and in processing it creatively. But they were much less happy about how much knowledge and insight the children had achieved about the way the E.C. functions. An open style of working does not appear to favour the attainment of this second objective. More direction was needed. The case study asks: 'Can one do something about European education in the primary school?' It answers:

European education in the sense of becoming conscious of differences and similarities between countries is certainly possible. The children were enthusiastically occupied, but trying to foster insight into the functioning of the E.C. and its agencies and the value of it for Member States appears to be aiming too high. It is too complicated and the children have too little knowledge at their disposal. It is better to try an example, e.g. co-operation between two countries in agriculture.

The study goes on to ask how one would develop such a project in the ordinary school day. The teacher researchers concluded: 'The two schools involved were well able to formulate and design this new curricular element'.

There were some pedagogical problems, e.g. a closed/open approach and some organisational problems e.g. the length of the project but 'these problems can be solved if there is a good team spirit, positive attitudes in all involved, flexibility of approach and thorough preparation so that parents are satisfied the children are learning'.

The action research unit at Mons concluded:

Our objectives were numerous. At the centre of our concern was, of course, Teaching about Europe in the Primary School. Here, we did not only want to develop knowledge about the Europe of the Twelve but, also, to reflect upon what it meant to teach in a European spirit. We wanted to live out democratic experiences, pluralistic open ones, linking practitioners in the school (nursery, primary, secondary, higher, be it University or not), responsible adults (management, inspectors, teachers, parents), children and post-secondary students, convinced Europeans and people of goodwill. We hoped to work with those responsible for primary teaching and to submit the results of our researches to criticism. We hoped to create a dynamic capable of setting in motion a mechanism of consciousness – raising participation that would not stop with the drawing up of the case study. We wanted to light the way for taking up responsibility for the future. We can claim that those objectives were pursued with enthusiasm and that they have been met broadly speaking. Involved in the Action Research were individuals or small groups who had a taste for research, who took pleasure in communicating their results, and who were curious about the discoveries of others.

The case study goes on to point out that the way the project developed in different institutions was influenced by geographical, socio-cultural and pedagogic factors. One difficulty with the global evaluation of the project was that it was not possible to get all the participants together in one place at the same time. The main theme of the study is that the political decision to bring about a European society has been taken and that teachers have a duty to prepare young minds for this reality. They can only do this, it is suggested, if they themselves are equipped for this responsibility right from the start of initial teacher training by a combination of theory and practice leading to an awareness of the nature of Europe and European choices. The authors conclude that 'Even though the general objectives of the Action Research have been attained globally in this project, the size of the task is such that it cannot be accomplished by the efforts of a few dedicated teachers'. The study concludes with a plea for a radical change in the training of all teachers to incorporate the European dimension.

The Nancy case study summarises successes and failures with children at different age levels. In the nursery classes, children showed great interest in bringing papers, documents, books, stamps and other things which they got from their parents. They were able to build up concepts from their activities. The teachers found that the scheme gave them considerable scope for action. The children enjoyed the European festival at Christmas and were reported to feel pride in associating with the older pupils and having their parents working with them in school . . . a rare event in France. But they had the usual difficulties over notions of geographical location and historical time. Further work was proposed more in keeping with the childrens' capabilities.

The lower primary classes were judged to be very much interested in the work and were eager to expand it. Finding sufficient information was a problem and one topic had to be abandoned for lack of material. In the upper primary classes, some mathematical and computer skills were mastered but others were not, partly due to lack of time and instructions being too complicated.

In the lower secondary school, the making of the Portuguese book was a great success. In the English lessons, the children not only acquired insight into life in another country and improved their standard of English but exhibited more positive attitudes to school work in general.

In the short term, it was concluded there were positive gains but in the longer term the weight of habit appeared to militate against the fulfilment of the original aspirations. For example training sessions in action research tended to be regarded as interludes in the daily routine. Participants found it difficult to get colleagues to share in their enthusiasm and the circulation of information about the project proved to be a poor substitute for actual involvement in the training sessions. It was suggested that a better match between training sessions and classroom practice should be sought by the more frequent use of action research in teacher training.

Summary evaluation

The project method of action research leading to the collaborative development of case studies proved to be generally effective not only for raising European awareness, but also for enhancing teaching skills. This was particularly evident where the support of related agencies, institutions and individuals were effectively co-ordinated by a sponsoring unit led by facilitators with substantial experience both of the processes of action research and the context of teaching about Europe. Problems arising from limited direct experience of European cultures among teachers and pupils showed that there was a need for substantial improvements in secondary sources. The use of electronic and other modern means of communication needed to be encouraged. More extensive use of networks and networking among European schools on a multilateral basis would have helped to develop the ethical aspects of the European dimension in the curriculum. Both issues I shall explore in greater detail later.

The general provision of training programmes for both facilitators and participants would have served the dual purpose of improving skills in the process of planning and evaluating change, and heightening awareness of managing thematic approaches for different ages and ability levels. The content of training workshops for similar projects in future should contain all these elements.

Attention has already been drawn to ways in which co-operation can be made to work including the involvement of adults other than teachers, especially parents. This factor I judge to be the single most important influence on the success of efforts to develop a European dimension of the curriculum. For example, there was mounting evidence that where a visitor to the classroom was a national of the country being studied by the class (whether a parent or not) there was a distinct tendency for there to be positive gains in attitudes and understanding by the pupils. The work of the European Parents' Association in support of the European dimension in schools is little known in the U.K. yet is well represented in certain parts of the European mainland. Bearing in mind that in the development of positive attitudes, the family has a crucial part to play (Macbeth *et al.*, 1984; Macbeth, 1989; Wolfendale, 1989) it is interesting to note how this point is reflected in one of 'ten principles' recently released by the

Association: 'School-learning and home learning should be recognised by all as contributory elements of education. The word "education" should not be used in official documents to denote schooling only'. (E.P.A. Special Bulletin, 1990)

Similarly at an earlier seminar held in Dublin on the parental contribution towards 1992, special reference was made to the training of teachers for working with parents (E.P.A., 1988). The outcomes of the Europe in the primary school project indicated specific ways in which such training could improve the development of a European dimension in home–school relations. It also illustrated a variety of approaches and starting points for structuring both teaching and training activities, e.g.:

- a single country study,
- a European theme,
- an inter-cultural approach (emphasising regional or ethnic groupings and the contribution to both national and international roles),
- a non-European introduction,
- a global/international entry with Europe seen in this perspective,
- an inter-disciplinary organisation of pupil learning, e.g. humanities/European/environmental studies,
- a subject based framework, e.g. history/geography/art/music.

It was quite clear that whether teachers were used to central direction (France/Germany/Italy) or were undergoing a period of rapid change as in the U.K., they needed help and support to interpret curricula and programmes of study.

Indicators of success in developing a European dimension other than those already mentioned were predictably enough centred on the resourcefulness showed by teachers in providing or drawing upon first hand experiences and direct contacts. The use of a variety of other media increased the effectiveness of teaching and learning. Planning joint programmes in a bilateral or multilateral framework gave good results when the barriers to achieving effective communications had been removed. Finally, two factors emerged as crucial to successful development; the management of topic and inter-disciplinary work and appropriately structured resources and materials. Both areas urgently need addressing in the years ahead by training and investment whether through official or commercial sources of support.

Pupils attitudes need modifying to recognise more clearly the interdependent connections between European cultures in a global perspective. The scale of this task merely serves to confirm the necessity for more and better educational efforts. Given the many alternative approaches available to develop a European dimension, collaborative action research (whilst not being free from drawbacks), does have distinct advantages. The 'Teaching about Europe in the primary school' project served to illustrate not only some problems and opportunities in curriculum development in the years ahead, but also demonstrated that an extended concept of 'Community' can be achieved among practitioners, pupils, parents and policy makers by adopting this framework for co-operation. This is a theme I shall revisit in chapter four. Such a conception of Europe is located at the polar opposite to the notion of a super-power E.C. bureaucracy in which there is an enfeebling loss of national sovereignty; an assertion I shall examine further in the concluding chapter. The more immediate question is whether the resources necessary to initiate, implement, maintain, evaluate and disseminate the outcomes of such efforts match this vision, especially in the context of radical change.

In the following chapter, I shall therefore attempt to place the experience of the project in the context of the National Curriculum. The main challenge I shall try to address is providing not simply a definition but a conceptual map of the European dimension in the curriculum of primary and middle schools. My main intention is to show in what ways a European theme is already a dimension of established practice in primary and middle schools and offer some pointers towards its maintenance and development.

CHAPTER 3

The National Curriculum and European Citizenship

> Education shall be directed to the full development of the human
> personality and to the strengthening of respect for human rights, and
> fundamental freedoms. It shall promote understanding, tolerance and
> friendship among all nations, racial and religious groups, and shall
> further the activities of the United Nations for the maintenance of
> peace. (United National Universal Declaration of Human Rights,
> 1948, article 26/2)

Jean Monnet the leading architect of the European Community, has
been quoted as saying that if he had been able to begin again he would
have started with education. Had he witnessed recent events in Eastern
Europe, he may well have been prompted to further thought. For
despite the most concerted efforts to socialise pupils into a particular
ideology, this could not prevent the collapse of a form of life based
upon it. Clearly, schools cannot alone and unaided compensate for
society. So in thinking about setting our sights on prospects for
educational theory and practice for 1992 and beyond, our targets need
to be selective. We must separate the desirable from the necessary and
conserve our energies.

I propose that the most basic question that has to be asked is, 'what
is the role of the school in securing the proper functioning of an
economic union?' I shall attempt a longer answer, but the shorter
version reduces to an assertion, 'to find effective ways of tempering the
antagonisms necessary for a commercial enterprise to succeed'. For
unlike a political and cultural union based upon democratic principles
in which freedom, equality, fraternity and justice are the defining
features, we are presently required to live with a logic in which
competition necessarily restricts opportunities for co-operation and

national identity is potentially in conflict with European identity.

It should come as no surprise to discover that there is ambivalence about the role of the school in supporting such a community of interests. For as we have seen, whilst steps have been taken to create a free market in which to trade goods, the counterpart of a common educational market in which cultural practices at the school level are collaboratively studied has not so far been sanctioned.

The Council of Europe in addressing this issue stresses the centrality of inter-cultural education which 'is meant to connote an active process of communication and interaction between cultures to the mutual enrichment of each' (Council of Europe, 1984).

'Active communication and interaction between cultures' suggests a rationale for teaching quite distinct from a curriculum underpinned by the dissemination of ideas determined by and selected from a single society. The sociological theory on which inter-cultural pedagogy is based is to do with organising cross-cultural participation and collaboration. The aim is the encouragement of agreements in judgements in order to develop a rational consensus on educational issues. In this way, inter-cultural education challenges existing assumptions where these are based upon the making of national or imperial mentalities. For it brings together three main processes of political socialisation; schooling, involving the compulsory initiation of a child into the rights and duties of a citizen in a host culture; acculturation, the process of intensifying cultural influence through mutual contact; and re-socialisation, the process of changing attitudes and beliefs amongst adults (Mangan, 1990). Put in more concrete terms, if a common educational community is to succeed then the European dimension needs to permeate all parts of the curriculum of schools and teacher training agencies in Member States, actions need to be taken to promote contacts between parents, pupils and teachers at the school level, and training needs to be provided in order that teachers who are challenged to manage these changes consider themselves to be properly supported (C.E.V.N.O., 1987).

Such a programme requires an underlying theory to inform its practice in order that some coherence might be brought to the aim of progressing from a pedagogy directed towards an economic union, to a philosophy of education which would encompass political and cultural union. Such an approach must succeed in integrating efforts to teach about Europe with the enterprise of becoming a European through the definition of common ground (Wilson and Cowell, 1982; Ryba, 1989).

Developing European citizenship

The conceptual model I shall offer as a starting point for reflection on these issues extends and develops the following commentary by a past President of the Association for Teacher Education in Europe concerning inter-cultural education:

> A critical awareness of cultural diversity and unity will have to permeate the curriculum. What we now need within the European Community is an education which prepares its citizens to become inter-cultural in the sense that they appreciate their true heritage as citizens of richly interacting societies in Europe. (Hellawell, 1986)

Similarly, a distinguished President of the Centre for European Education in Italy recently commented that 'we need to develop all over the world, but chiefly in the most advanced countries both action and research in cross curricular activities which give a structure to peace education' (Visalberghi, 1989). I propose that such a structure for cross-curricular activities can be represented as seven overlapping processes, see figure 3.1.

Education for personal identity acknowledges that a central feature of political socialisation must be a well formed self concept. *Education for national identity* places the pupils' self concept in the perspective of a multi-cultural society. *Education for inter-cultural understanding* modulates personal and collective identities by exposing the experiences of these societies to the possibility of other equally worthwhile ways of life. *Education for European citizenship* when related to *education for economic and industrial understanding* offers opportunities for practising the skills of inter-cultural participation through the living example of a Community whose regulative framework of laws and conventions are designed to empower its citizens and to protect its environment. And *education for international understanding* in combination with *education for the global environment* acts as a corrective to Euro-centrism by demonstrating the interdependent nature of European and global citizenship.

This conceptual map offers a structure for developing the knowledge, skills and attitudes necessary to underpin the European dimension of the curriculum in a framework which provides linkage with the development of European citizenship. It also implies that the achievement of political literacy through inter-cultural education is not confined to secondary pupils or adults. It properly accommodates interventions in the early years when attitudes to self are formed and when an opportunity exists for holistic teaching freed from the

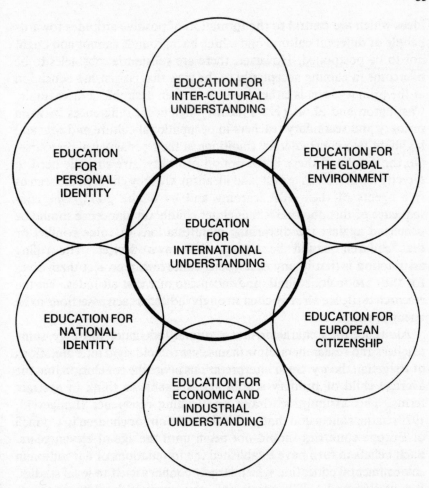

Figure 3.1 Developing a European dimension

constraints of examination subjects and multiple mentors. Support for such a standpoint emerges from international studies of socialisation patterns which clearly demonstrate the importance of the ages three to thirteen in developing ethnocentric attitudes (Hess and Torney, 1965; Lambert and Klineberg, 1967; Massialas, 1972). The development of positive self regard, effective communication skills and the ability to co-operate – all essential enabling conditions for inter-cultural education – are significantly influenced by teaching and training in the primary school (Fountain and Selby, 1988).

All of this evidence suggests that the basic concepts of similarity and difference, continuity and change, reciprocity and inter-dependence, ideas which are central to the formation of positive attitudes towards people of different cultural and ethnic backgrounds cannot and ought not to be postponed. However, there are substantial obstacles to be overcome in gaining acceptance of the view that citizenship education at the primary level is either possible or even desirable. For example, Carrington and Short (1987) identify significant differences between primary and secondary teachers in occupational culture and role and highlight two contradictory traditions in their pedagogical discourse. On the one hand there is the notion of utility, stressing the need to directly teach what is useful, and idealism whereby children are seen as free agents of their own learning and by nature good. One consequence of this doctrine is that either childhood innocence should be protected against the disturbing manifestations of value conflict or that children should be left to their own devices. The ruling assumption is that in any case young children can protect themselves for they are 'colour blind' and incapable of racist attitudes. Yet the research evidence already cited strongly indicates such assertions to be unsupported.

Alongside these characteristics of primary education ideology, some teachers and researchers show themselves to hold rigid interpretations of Piagetian theory. Such interpretations invite the conclusion that the average child of primary school age is unable to think in abstract terms. This assumption draws one leading researcher (Langeveld, 1979) to the conclusion that political education for children in Council of Europe countries should not begin until the age of eleven years. Such beliefs in turn have established the foundations of a tradition in environmental education which largely confines itself to local studies. But as Weigand (1990) points out, two recent School Inspectorate reports in England and Wales have shown that the study of unfamiliar places deserved greater attention than it is often given and comments on the almost total absence of a national and world dimension to the work inspected in history and geography. Both findings highlight the need for British primary schools to consider a broader perspective (D.E.S., 1986; H.M.I., 1989). Such problems are not however confined to England and Wales. For example, Mickel (1986) comments that even in the average three year compulsory vocational school in the former Federal Republic of Germany with one weekly class of politics, there can be no guarantee that topics dealing with European unification will be covered. Such resistance at the micro level of pedagogical theory is intensified at the macro level by the standpoint taken by several Member States, namely that the further down the education system educational interventions are proposed, the greater the presumed interference in national sovereignty. Overcoming such self defeating impediments to education for European citizenship must become a priority for 1992 and beyond for as a result of them, the European dimension of the primary school curriculum in particular has become marginalised, depreciated and neglected.

The problem of method

In remedying these deficiencies, I suggest that specific consideration needs to be given to the methods through which citizenship education should be taught.[1]

A recent study in the U.K. commissioned by the Speaker of the House of Commons arose out of just such a concern that young people should know how they are governed and be able to participate in their society 'irrespective of the course of study being followed, and from the earliest years of schooling' (H.M.S.O., 1990). The Commission's recommendation emphasises the skills of citizenship as crucial to the success of such an enterprise. They advocate that schools should offer opportunities for pupils to learn how to express opposition fairly, effectively and peacefully through participating in debate and elections, though representing the viewpoints of others, by working on projects collaboratively, and by engaging in voluntary activity which brings them into closer contact with the local community. The National Curriculum Council, taking into account the work of the Speaker's Commission, recently published its views on ways in which education for citizenship might be strengthened and ensured in every school (N.C.C., 1990d). Its place in the curriculum is described as one of five:

> cross-curricular themes . . . [which] . . . share common features e.g. the capacity to promote discussion of values and beliefs, to extend knowledge and understanding, to encourage practical activities and decision making, and to strengthen the bond between the individuals and the community. (N.C.C., 1990d: 1)

Reference is made to the survey undertaken on behalf of the Speakers Commission which showed that 67 per cent of schools contacted had no agreed policy or curriculum document in this area of the curriculum. The N.C.C. comments:

> No doubt many cover it in time-honoured ways – civics, political education, personal and social education, through immersion in the

corporate life of the school. All of these are valid; *in future there must be a guarantee that they combine to form a rational entitlement.* (my emphasis)

The N.C.C. omitted to mention that the survey was restricted to a random sample of 800 maintained secondary schools and elicited a response rate of slightly more than half (455 returns: 57 per cent). While the researcher (Fogelman, 1990) considered this response rate to be 'very satisfactory', this seems debateable when judged against the uses to which such a statistic verified in this way was later put. Moreover, it is difficult to understand why such a useful survey was so limited in its application. For as it stands, the strategy adopted by the Speaker's Commission as later adapted by the N.C.C., is significantly weakened by its assumption that a proper knowledge base is defined in terms of pupils aged eleven years and over. It thus omits to give due weight and consideration to the 30,000 nursery, infant, junior and middle state schools in England and Wales who might well have merited consultation. This seems an ironic disenfranchisement of a large proportion of its potential constituency.

Happily, both the Speaker's Commission first recommendation that 'the study and experience of citizenship should be a part of every young person's education from the earliest years of schooling' and the N.C.C.'s outline of activities, opportunities and experiences extending across all key stages from 1 to 4 suggest that such an interpretation would not be intended. The study of controversial issues, particularly by children in the middle years of schooling (seven to thirteen years), is especially crucial in the effective delivery of a programme which successfully integrates the seven inter-linked components I have outlined for developing a European dimension. This factor is specifically highlighted by the N.C.C. in its commentary on 'Teaching for Citizenship' where it acknowledges the need for 'pupils to have the opportunity to acquire knowledge, to develop respect for evidence, to clarify their own values, and to understand that people hold different, equally legitimate points of view'. In drawing attention to the legislation of the Education Act (1986) which obliges Local Education Authorities, governing bodies and headteachers:

> to forbid partisan political activities in primary schools, and the promotion of partisan political views in the teaching of any subject in all schools. Where political issues are brought to the attention of pupils, there is also a duty to ensure that they are offered a balanced presentation of opposing views. (N.C.C., 1990d)

The principles of procedure which would ensure this effect are not made clear. The overwhelming concentration of attention is on content and not process. A significant indicator of process is provided by the N.C.C. in the matter of European Citizenship:

> Curriculum provision should build on personal experiences and encourage pupils to see citizenship as something which extends beyond their immediate experiences and relationships. Individuals have obligations to and relationships with national, European and world-wide communities. Citizens in the 1990s and beyond will require an appreciation of the significance of the economic, social and political changes taking place in Europe and of the need for international co-operation. (N.C.C., 1990d: 15)

For an international review of these issues, the work of Flouris and Spiridakis (1988) provides an exhaustive survey of teaching styles, classroom organisation and curriculum materials in social studies curricula. They conclude that 'the school, as well as other traditional socialising agents, directly or indirectly promote conformity, passivity, ethnocentrism, patriotism, parochial pedagogy and negative geopolitical sentiments instead of internationalism, cosmopolitanism, and global awareness.

There is an urgent need to clarify and elaborate alternative role models for the teacher in order to improve the quality teaching of controversial issues (Calogiannakis-Hourdakis, 1988). In this connection the concept of the 'neutral' teacher (Elliott, 1975) might usefully be re-examined. The revised concept, perhaps of the 'impartial' teacher would act as a counter-balance to the tendencies already noted for an institutional framework to arise in which dependency relationships are linked to hierarchies. In such circum-stances, there is a tendency for truth to be determined not by reference to evidence, but finally by deference to persons by virtue of role. This situation effectively sets the truth of power against the power of truth and results in what Foucault has described as 'power knowledge' (Foucault, 1977; Couzens Hoy, 1986; Whitehead, 1989; Ball, 1990; Sheridan, 1980).

The main corrective to such conceptions of pedagogy is to find more and better ways of encouraging critical dialogue and critical thinking – a theme I shall return to. In this way, a re-interpretation of the concept of the 'whole curriculum' emerges. For not only is there the requirement to integrate core and foundation subjects and cross-curricular dimensions and themes, there is a recognition of the need to co-ordinate didactic and enquiry styles of teaching and learning. The concept of 'wholeness' refers to the effective delivery of each.

The German philosopher, Habermas, has provided a penetrating account of how such an aspiration must necessarily be achieved by analysing the conditions under which truth arises in discourse. Thus, the 'ideal' classroom organisation for the purpose of studying controversial issues is formally defined in terms of certain requirements being met namely when:

(i) participants enter dialogue under conditions of equal opportunity;
(ii) power relations are neutralised through an over-riding aim to pursue truth;
(iii) participants have the same chances to raise issues, make proposals, call into question, sufficient to leave no assertion free from critical examination.
(iv) discussion is sufficiently free from the distorting influence of group organisation to enable a rational consensus to arise. (McCarthy, 1978)

For our purposes, 'participants' would not, however be restricted to teachers and pupils. As we have already seen, the community of enquirers would encompass all those whose activities are deemed to be formative in the conception of a European dimension and whose contribution is being studied or whose views are being sought. For these reasons the study of value conflict should be planned preferably with parental involvement and on a whole school basis. A proposed strategy for managing this will provide the main focus of the following chapter. The central purpose of the general approach should be to ensure that those issues that are considered 'dangerous' (and European unity is but one) should not be avoided, to do so would be to school or indoctrinate as distinct from educate. Indeed a central issue for citizenship education must be training in the skills of critical dialogue in a framework in which controversial issues are controlled, if not finally settled, through experiencing democratic teaching situations in a setting characterised by equal opportunities (Antonouris and Wilson, 1989).

Stenhouse (1969), commenting on the nature of this kind of open-minded teaching proposes that our 'strategy must renounce the position of a teacher as an "expert" capable of solving by authority all issues about values that arise in discussion – because this position cannot be logically justified'. A common core curriculum in citizenship education agreed at European level, which incorporated such features, would greatly assist in resolving many of these difficulties. It would also have the advantage of facilitating the study in initial and in-service teacher training courses of the processes of political socialis-ation. This in turn may yield a more informed view of the possibilities as well as the limits of schooling. Similarly, a common handbook for teachers in training might assist in improving student performance on teaching practice. This would address the deficiency which was identified in a recent survey of U.K. teacher training institutions concerning provision for the European dimension (Convey, 1988).

Such moves towards a common core curriculum of the European dimension are not so unthinkable for a plan for the development of international understanding has already been approved by U.N.E.S.C.O. since November 1985 (see also Goodson *et al.*, 1984; Goodson and McGivney, 1985). Moreover, at least one European country (the former Federal Republic of Germany) as long ago as 1978 attempted to define what counts as the European dimension in order to assist coherence and consistency of effort in a pluralistic situation. The minimum objectives required by constituent Ministries were as follows:

- a willingness to promote communication, work to overcome prejudices and acknowledge similarities, all the while affirming the diversity of Europe;
- the development of European legal ties within the framework of the principles and goals of the European Human Rights Convention and Social Charter;
- a view towards neighbourly togetherness and the readiness to enter into compromises for the realisation of different interests in Europe;
- the realisation of human rights, equal opportunities and economic, social and legal security and freedom of movement;
- the safeguarding of peace in Europe and the World. (Mickel, 1986)

The study of controversial issues and teaching European citizenship within the framework I have put forward for developing a European dimension reduces to an essential pre-condition; the establishment of a policy within a whole school curriculum strategy.

From reflection to action: the development of policy at national and local level

Pointers to progress in developing policy statements and models in a U.K. context can be gleaned from a pilot project among twelve Local Education Authorities. The two-year project aimed to raise European awareness in all types of educational institutions (Central Bureau, 1990). The experience of the project provides insights into the context and function of policy guidelines, the nature of European awareness, how it might be delivered, and the factors enabling and inhibiting its development. The suggested framework to emerge for L.E.A.s seeking to develop policy guidelines for European awareness is outlined as follows:

- a statement of overall aims related to a definition of and rationale for European awareness based on existing practice;
- a statement of the potential contribution made by a range of subjects and areas of the curriculum to European awareness;
- examples of experiences within the U.K. which can contribute to European awareness;
- examples of experiences in other European countries which contribute to European awareness;
- a list of available resources including information technology, organisations and their addresses, publications and sources of funding;
- practical guidelines for planning visits;
- a phased and costed programme of in-service training to support the future development of European awareness;
- a list of people within an authority, either commercial or members of working parties, with the specific task of supporting and developing European awareness. Such a list will offer evidence not only of commitment but of the width of interest within the educational service, for example, from pre-school to adult education and including special needs, the youth service, further and higher education, but also areas of support from outside the education system, for example, the offices of chief executives, chambers of commerce, treasurers departments, town twinning committees and employers. (Central Bureau, 1990)

Commenting on factors enabling European awareness, the report highlights the importance of the Education Committee of L.E.A.s giving an unambiguous lead. Town twinnings, links with media, and for older pupils work experience and work shadowing, facilitate development as do working and task groups that not only draw their members from advisory and inspection services and teachers in primary and secondary schools, but also have representatives from teacher training, further and higher education, the youth service and adult education. Access to documentation, effective dissemination and evaluated experience, databases of resources and materials, the use of language assistants and advisory teachers, the use of information technology, earmarked funding, and knowledge of schemes, awards and services, (from organisations such as the Central Bureau for Educational Visits and Exchanges and the Council of Europe) were all additional and enabling factors.

Among the inhibiting influences on the development of European awareness were instanced the current overload in schools arising from introducing the National Curriculum, shortage of resources, relevant in-service training, time for developing contacts and especially visits and exchanges, and not least the personal costs accruing to teachers who attempt to organise bilateral or multilateral activities. All of these matters need to be taken account of in the development of school based policies. The N.C.C. suggest that this process can be facilitated by selective use of the following five steps:

- discuss objectives,
- identify possible ways of teaching,
- analyse the readiness of the school,
- decide policy,
- plan implementation.

Chief amongst the early considerations in discussing objectives will be the formulation of a definition. Three recent U.K. examples can be drawn upon from the D.E.S., N.C.C. and the Central Bureau to supplement or adapt the statement of objectives already agreed upon by the E.C. as quoted in chapter one.

(1) *D.E.S., February 1991, The Objectives of the European Dimension in Education*:
The Government has been and will continue to be active in promoting the objectives of the E.C. resolution on the European dimension in education. The Government's policies are aimed at:

- helping pupils and students to acquire a view of Europe as a multi-cultural, multi-lingual community which includes the U.K.;
- encouraging awareness of the variety of European histories, geographies and cultures;
- preparing young people to take part in the economic and social development of Europe and making them aware of the opportunities and challenges that arise;
- encouraging interest in and improving competence in other European languages;
- imparting knowledge of political, economic and social developments, past, present and future, including knowledge about the origins, workings and role of the E.C.;
- promoting a sense of European identity, through first hand experience of other countries where appropriate;
- promoting an understanding of the E.C.'s interdependence with the rest of Europe, and with the rest of the world. (D.E.S., 1991)

(2) *N.C.C. November 1990, Report of Sub-Task Group on the European Dimension in Education*:
The European dimension in education should enable pupils to live and work with a degree of competence in other European countries, to reflect critically on experience in them so as to give an informed understanding of the predicaments and aspirations of other Europeans in order to reflect critically on or challenge existing perceptions. (N.C.C., 1990e)

(3) *Central Bureau, June 1990, European Awareness Pilot Project Final Report*:
European awareness seeks to help all young people to see themselves in a European context and to help as many as possible to live and work with some confidence in other European countries, to reflect critically on the experiences in them so as to give them a more informed understanding of the predicament and aspirations of fellow Europeans so that at the same time they can better understand and develop their own. (Central Bureau, 1990: para 5.4).

Such statements at a national level within England and Wales can be compared with a recent statement of the Standing Conference of the Ministers of Education and Cultural Affairs of the former Federal Republic of Germany (1990). Under the terms of the West German constitution, each region exercised autonomy in its educational administration and organisation. The U.K. equivalent to this statement would be a common agreement amongst all L.E.A.s in England and Wales, Scotland and Northern Ireland about the place of what is defined as 'Europe in the Classroom'. The policy statement begins with a section entitled *The Political Starting Point*:

> Europe is more than just a geographical term. Europe in all its dimensions embraces a common historical heritage, a common cultural tradition and, to an increasing extent, a common perception of reality. The painful experiences of two World Wars as well as the development in Western and Eastern Europe since 1945 have given the Europeans every reason to reflect upon their common origins and in recognition of the fact that they belong together to embark upon new avenues towards co-operation and unification.

It continues:

> The goal is the creation of a European union. Part of this perspective in the long term is the notion of a common European house, in which all countries and peoples will be able to achieve self determination and freedom. At the same time it is essential, also and in particular against the background of the process of German unification, to create a

Europe with federal structures, which guarantees the preservation of cultural peculiarities, social diversity, a balanced economic development and grass roots decision making Member States.

And the statement concludes:

The process of European integration challenges Europeans to see their national history and traditions in a new light, to appreciate other people's perspectives, to be tolerant, to express solidarity and to practice co-existence with people who speak different languages and have other customs. Europeans must recognise the responsibility for freedom, peace, justice and social balance placed in their hands – above all with regard to the developing countries. (Standing Conference, 1990).

Turning to the application of these political principles in schools, the following policy guidelines are provided:

European Awareness as a Pedagogical Assignment of the School
The school has the task of making the European peoples and countries aware of the integration process and the realignment of their relations. It is intended to make a contribution towards developing awareness of European identity and fostering understanding of the fact that in many spheres of our lives European terms of reference apply and that European decisions are necessary. (Standing Conference, 1990)

In order to realise this European dimension in teaching and education, the school has to convey knowledge and views on:

- the geographical diversity of the European region as a result of its natural, social and economic structures,
- the political and social structures of Europe,
- the formative historical forces in Europe, above all the development of the European views on law, the state and freedom,
- the patterns of development, features and evidence of what is despite its variety a common European culture,
- the multi-lingual nature of Europe and its inherent cultural wealth,
- the history of the European idea and the attempts at integration since 1945,
- the harmonisation of interest and joint action in Europe towards solving economic, ecological, social and political problems,
- the tasks and working methods of European institutions.

The basic values of state, social and individual life on which the teaching and educational aims of the school orient themselves must be seen in their relationship to life in the European community of peoples and states. This involves:

- the willingness to reach understanding so as to overcome prejudice and to be able to recognise mutual interests whilst at the same time affirming European diversity,
- an open-minded attitude to culture which transcends cultural borders yet preserves individual cultural identity,
- respect for the values of European legal commitments and the administration of justice within the framework of human rights recognised in Europe,
- the ability to coexist as neighbours and the willingness to make compromises regarding the realisation of the different interests in Europe, even when this involves sacrifice for the benefit of others,
- support for freedom, democracy, human rights, justice and economic security,
- the will to maintain peace in Europe and throughout the world.

These then are some recent policy statements from England, Wales and Germany which can be compared with those emanating from the E.C. However, the possibility inherent in the informal curriculum should not be overlooked in developing policies, particularly where additional resources can be found perhaps through the involvement of parents and adults other than teachers.

In the welter of change currently affecting schools, the consequent timetable pressures arising, and in view of recent changes in the conditions of service for teachers, it seems almost quaint to talk of extra curricular activities. An outstanding example of the success of such initiatives can, nevertheless, be found in a relatively new Member State's programme for the European dimension. In the space of approximately three years, the Ministry of Education in Portugal has established over 400 European clubs in schools and colleges and produced three packs of teaching materials to support this work. A clearer understanding of the potential of such clubs can be gathered from a reading of their constitution:

EUROPEAN CLUBS
(1)   European Clubs are centres designed to facilitate activities concerning European education.
(2)   European Clubs are set up according to proposals of primary and secondary schools which define their context, conditions and possibilities.
(3)   Pupils and teachers are free to join these Clubs.
(4)   Aims and objectives of European Clubs are stated as follows:

       (a) to create among their members a truly European spirit to be spread, by all possible means, among the members of the community to which they belong;

(b) to promote, with the support of the competent institutions, activities that may provide better information about:

- Europe (geographical, historical, cultural, economic features, etc.).
- European institutions (structure, functions, objectives, etc.)
- The Member States of the E.C. and of the Council of Europe (politics, social and cultural life, etc.).
- Cultural and natural European heritage.
- Main issues that address the challenge of defining a contemporary Europe.
- Objectives of European integration.

(c) to contribute towards comprehension of pluralism – similarities and differences;

(d) to contribute towards understanding and tolerance;

(e) to promote awareness of European international interdependence and necessary co-operation;

(f) to imbue pupils and young people with a sense of responsibility as European citizens, especially with regard to peace, human rights and preservation of the environment and the cultural heritage.

(5) In order to carry out these actions European Clubs shall engage in activities such as:

(a) collecting documentation and updated information generally accessible;

(b) organising meetings, colloquies, etc;

(c) projecting films lent by E.C. institutions, embassies, etc., which may promote a better knowledge and understanding of the Community, the Council of Europe and of different countries of Europe;

(d) spreading information about and participating in activities which may contribute towards introduction of European dimension in education, namely Europe at School – European Schools' Day Competition;

(e) organising and participating in cultural activities, competitions and exhibitions for the purpose of improving knowledge of European realities;

(f) organisation of Europe's Week and Member States Weeks dedicated to each Member State of the Community and Council of Europe;

(g) exchange of information and documentation among national Clubs and possibly other Member States' Clubs or schools;

(h) organisation of visits to national Clubs and similar Clubs or schools in the Member States;

(i) production and development of teaching materials, games, puzzles, journals, etc.

(6)   Each European Club may elaborate its own regulations provided that it fits into this general conception.

(7)   Each European Club may devise its own badge as well as its own motto. (Ministry of Education, Centre for European Education, Lisbon, Portugal)

Policy in action

An example of a developed policy document at the local level in England can be found in Sheffield L.E.A.s, 'The European Dimension Statement'.[2] This document provides a practical and comprehensive handbook for developing the European dimension within one L.E.A. Its outline of aims includes the following:

To enable all Europeans;
● to develop lively enquiring minds, an ability to question and discuss rationally;
● to develop the social, communication and study skills that will enable an individual to act autonomously and co-operatively with others;
● to develop and clarify their own values and attitudes and to be sure of the values and attitudes of others;
● to develop an understanding of key concepts, areas of knowledge, principles and values relevant to the human condition to enable Europeans to interpret the world in which they live and gain a vision of the future. (Sheffield L.E.A., 1990a)

A similar most useful initiative, taken by Humberside County Council provides a guide for schools and colleges in their efforts to raise levels of European awareness. Its structure includes some helpful suggestions about the role of school based co-ordinators. Large schools in particular may benefit from this type of appointment and where clusters or families of schools collaborate, a co-ordinator for European awareness may be considered to be a significantly enabling factor in achieving success.[3] It is suggested for example that in general, such an appointment would:

● heighten the level of awareness of Europe throughout the school (or cluster of schools),
● support colleagues in their guidance of pupils in the way in which they relate to people from other European countries,
● help pupils appreciate the potential careers, opportunities offered by the Single European Market.

In particular the activities of a European co-ordinator would:

- contribute towards a school policy statement on European awareness which may be included in the school management plan,
- conduct a curriculum audit for European awareness and communicate the results to the appropriate staff committee and to the governing body,
- emphasise the importance of a second language,
- seek additional cross-curricular applications for European awareness by liaising with all staff/departments/other schools,
- on occasion provide an input into school-based I.N.S.E.T.,
- create a resource bank of support materials which may be accessed by any department or used in P.S.E., e.g. videos, magazines, posters, artifacts,
- oversee a European noticeboard to provide a changing display of (e.g.) European sport, jobs vacant, media events,
- monitor and support existing exchanges and links with other European schools and encourage participation and follow-up work by as many departments as possible,
- establish new links and exchanges which involve as many pupils as possible,
- research the European involvement of local industry and invite industrialists and other appropriate speakers into school,
- monitor and evaluate cross-curricular developments in relation to European awareness in the curriculum,
- be aware and make use of L.E.A. initiatives on European awareness and provide feedback on school activities,
- monitor publications from national organisations and institutions and exploit the material that they offer, e.g. Central Bureau, U.K. Centre for European Education, European Parliament and Commission,
- co-ordinate European special event/evening/day,
- where appropriate oversee the founding and running of a European Club or when liaising with secondary schools or colleges, to link with a European Society perhaps using the guidelines produced by the Industrial Society for Sixth Form European Societies.

A further helpful analysis of possibilities contained in the same document indicates possible links with the National Curriculum (see Appendix 3).

Another example of policy development at the local level in a different sense i.e. based on a cluster of schools, arose from a collaborative action research project in three Doncaster schools in partnership with the L.E.A. Advisory Service, the Doncaster Teaching Support Service, Schools Library Service and Nottingham Polytechnic's Centre for European Education.[4] The significance of this particular initiative was its concern with bringing together external consultants and existing sources of support in a co-ordinated way. The main aims of the project were to relate the European dimension to the National Curriculum within the schools' overall curriculum planning, to create appropriate teaching resources and evaluate teaching materials developed through the E.C. 'Europe in the Primary School' project.

Three schools were involved; a first, junior and middle school from different types of catchment area. They worked co-operatively to explore the aims of the project which they expressed in the following terms:

In general we would be seeking to develop:

● positive attitudes towards the cultural and ethnic SIMILARITIES and DIFFERENCES of our European neighbours,
● an understanding of the VALUES and BELIEFS of various peoples including such aspects as food, festivals and way of life,
● an appreciation of the INTERDEPENDENCE of the European nations upon each others
● an interest in and awareness of LOCATION and COMMUNICATION in terms of places, boundaries and geographical features,
● a knowledge of CHANGE from the co-incidental upheavals in Eastern Europe during the course of the project (1989–90). (Doncaster L.E.A./Nottingham Polytechnic, 1990)

The outcomes of this project included a joint statement by the schools of their key objectives for European work in the primary curriculum:

KEY POLICY OBJECTIVES FOR EUROPEAN WORK IN THE PRIMARY CURRICULUM
(1) To stimulate an awareness of, and an interest in our European neighbours, preferably through a cross-curricular theme.
(2) To encourage the formation of positive attitudes towards people of different cultural and ethnic backgrounds through the ideas of Similarity and Difference, Continuity and Change and Inter-dependence.
(3) To ensure sound school curriculum planning, bearing in mind national curriculum requirements and the individual needs of the children.

MAIN STRATEGIES FOR IMPLEMENTING POLICY
(1) To deliver the policies which are based on first-hand experience through a child-centred approach in line with best primary practice. Making use, wherever possible, of opportunities offered locally.

(2) To be aware of the development of teamwork, co-operation and liaison between all staff involved in the project.

(3) To make use of secondary resources such as Visitors, Contacts, Videos, Films, Media, Computer Software, Embassies, Tourist Offices and Travel Agents, etc. wherever possible, and to maintain a resourceful outlook for other opportunities.

DISSEMINATION
Display work in school and beyond.

A teacher check list of questions was also developed (mainly from a geographical standpoint) to be used before considering the European aspect of any proposed topic. Its purpose was to give the teacher ideas for possible approaches to studying the European dimension:

(1)   Do the children have an understanding of the shape of our world?
(2)   Do they have some concept of the meaning of the word 'continents'. Can they recognise and name the continents and oceans of the world?
(3)   Do they understand about the poles and equator and the conditions found in those regions?
(4)   Do they know where Europe is in relation to the other continents, poles, equator, Atlantic Ocean and Mediterranean?
(5)   Do they know where the British Isles are within Europe?
(6)   Do they know what countries make up the United Kingdom?
(7)   Do they know where London is within England?
(8)   Do they know where Doncaster is within Great Britain?
(9)   Do they understand basic directions?

Obviously the answers to these questions will depend upon the age and abilities of the classes being questioned. However, from the answers given, the teacher may glean some awareness of the geographical concept of Europe understood by the class. Armed with this knowledge, the teacher will then have to decide the best method of approach for aiding the class with a wider awareness of our European neighbours. The approach taken may be from the local to the regional to international or vice versa. Some necessary visual aids will of course be a globe, a world map and a map of Europe.

An extension of the above check list to incoporate other curriculum subjects and cross-curricular themes, may be developed from the following outline:

DIAGNOSING EUROPEAN AWARENESS
The questions below are indicative and incomplete and are not presented in any order of priority.

(1) Enhancing language capability to facilitate communication and co-operation.

    (a) What modern European languages are taught within the school?

    (b) What language awareness teaching is being undertaken to compensate for identified gaps?

    (c) What modern language skills can be accessed amongst staff, pupils and parents?

    (d) What resources are available to support language capability programmes?

(2) Appreciation of historical, cultural, social, economic and scientific achievements of other European countries.

    (a) What specific and major achievements have each of the European countries made to the development of the ways of life in the U.K. today?

    (b) What are the main regional sub-divisions of Europe?

    (c) Which country has the highest/lowest income per head of population?

    (d) What contacts exist amongst the staff, pupils, governing body?

(3) Awareness of and tolerance towards cultural, religious, social, geographical and linguistic diversity.

    (a) What are the population and land area statistics for each European country?

    (b) Where are the main topographical features of Europe?

    (c) What are the main religious and ethnic groups?

    (d) What are the main and lesser used languages and where can they be found?

    (e) Can you identify one main tradition or national holiday for each of the European countries, past or present?

(4) Knowledge of European political structures

    (a) What countries comprise the Council of Europe?

    (b) What is N.A.T.O./O.E.C.D./U.N.E.S.C.O.?

    (c) What is the Nordic Council?

    (d) What is the European Community?

    (e) What is E.F.T.A.?

    (f) What is the U.S.S.R.?

    (g) Where is the European Parliament, how is its membership elected and what is its present composition?

    (h) Where and what is the European Court of Justice; what are its functions and powers?

    (i) What are the main programmes of support available in the field of education, training and youth?

(5)   Awareness of current issues in Europe.

  (a) What are the main trends in European integration?
  (b) What are the major issues concerning integration occupying each of the countries of Europe today?
  (c) What are the main sources of information on European current affairs?
  (d) What opportunities exist for young people under the provisions of the single European Market?
  (e) What means are available to young people to secure the opportunities available to them?

Further insights into school based policies to develop a European dimension can be gained from the evaluated experience of 47 teachers, advisers, inspectors, trainers and other educationalists who attended a European awareness workshop jointly organised in October 1990 by the Central Bureau and Nottingham Polytechnic's Centre for European Education. Twenty-four L.E.A.s were represented, 21 from England and one each from Wales, Scotland and Northern Ireland. Subjects and areas represented included primary, secondary, post-16, T.V.E.I., modern languages, information technology, humanities, media education, communications and co-ordinators for European awareness. Key issues were seen to cluster around raising teacher awareness, providing appropriate resourcing, recognising interdependence, permeating the National Curriculum, and understanding and communicating the European dimension.

Using a collaborative evaluation procedure, three groups of participants considered the question as to what steps in the light of these key issues, should be taken in their own situation to further develop the European dimension. Rank ordered priorities for each group are listed below.

Group 1

(1)   The need to survey current involvement and practice nationwide, compile a national database of activities, and disseminate information and enthusiasm from this workshop.
(2)   The need for a greater and more explicit commitment from central government to the European dimension.
(3)   The need for coherent staff development policies including transnational collaboration.
(4)   The need to facilitate whole school involvement through school development plans incorporating European awareness as a whole school policy and the practical implementation of it.

(5) Committed and continued funding to enable all young people to experience first-hand contact with other Europeans.

Group 2

(1) The world and I – relationships.
(2) Resourced child-centred processes.
(3) Rights of access to information
(4) Operational framework policies, clarifying the curriculum, the 'Trojan Mouse' approach.

Group 3

(1) Importance of communication at all levels.
(2) Need for European awareness but built into a wider education policy including the national curriculum.
(3) Need for information, resources, support.
(4) Importance of first-hand experience.
(5) Need for realistic targets.

Summary rationale

I have presented a case for developing a European dimension based upon seven inter-related areas of knowledge and experience. Each of these areas; personal and national identity, citizenship, education for the global environment, economic and industrial understanding, inter-cultural and international education are processes which underlie the National Curriculum. This organisation of teaching and learning is interpreted as a whole curriculum in which core and foundation subjects are made relevant to pupils' lives through paying due regard to certain cross-curricular themes.

Such an analysis for developing a European dimension indicates that 'good' primary and middle schools will be doing this all the time. But like our use of language, we may take this for granted to a dangerous degree. Dangerous in the sense that concepts, skills and attitudes are insecurely caught; they also need to be taught. And whilst the National Curriculum programmes of study will remove ambiguity about 'what' needs to be taught, 'how' these subjects and the related themes are taught will require reflection if good primary teaching is going to prevail over the restricted competencies which subject chauvinism would engender in pupils and staff alike.

Critical reflection will certainly be required on old habits if the European dimension is to be realised. Critical attention in particular will have to be paid to the weaknesses as much as the strengths of child-centred theory, the management of topic and project work, the involvement of adults other than teachers including parents, the traditional insularity of the British way of life, the place of citizenship in the personal and social education of pupils, the relation of Europe to Commonwealth and world affairs, and not least the pedagogy of controversial issues including the vexed question of the quality of the global environment.

In order for these profound and troubling concerns to be brought into the ownership of the school and its community, I have emphasised that the European dimension should become part of the school development plan. A whole school policy statement will be necessary as a first step in developing teaching for and about Europe.

A study of policy models will help to raise levels of European awareness to the point where the unique circumstances of every school will assert themselves. A statement of policy at this point will help to clarify a commitment that will command support amongst those who have been consulted and develop understanding amongst staff who are to act on its principles. It may then provide a benchmark for evaluated experience to be progressively built up, and under appropriate circumstances provide the foundation for action research based teaching.

From policy to practice: case histories of developing a European dimension

The European dimension is at one and the same time present in schools yet hard to detect. This ambiguous situation is both a strength and a weakness. It is a strength in that by permeating all parts of the curriculum, it takes a proportionate place in the delivery of a whole curriculum. It stands as a weakness in that the relevant knowledge, skills and attitudes are difficult to monitor and evaluate. For similar reasons, the transfer of experience from one practitioner to another in order to strengthen theory and practice is presently poorly developed.

In what follows, I shall offer examples of current practice to illustrate some problems and opportunities in developing a European dimension.

Case history 1: the school link

Chris Truman, headteacher of a Church Aided junior school with 125 pupils on roll agreed to take part in the evaluation of teaching materials developed through the 'Europe in the Primary School' project. In a village setting on the fringes of a large conurbation, it has five class groups aged five to eleven years. The school was visited in 1988 by the national co-ordinators of the European dimension in Portugal. Supported by the governors, the school agreed to form a link with a large urban school in Portugal. Towards the end of February 1989, a box was delivered by post from Lisbon. It contained Christmas greetings and teaching materials including jigsaws of Portugal, 3D figures dressed in regional costume, and audio tapes of Portuguese phrases. It also contained a message which announced an intention to make a visit to England in June.

With the assistance of the U.K. Central Bureau and at the invitation of the Ministry of Education in Portugal, the headteacher visited the link school in May to see a European Club in action and make final arrangements for receiving pupils, staff and parents at his school.

Staying at a local youth hostel, the party of 28 pupils and 17 adults were welcomed after a marathon coach journey from Lisbon via Paris and London. A joint programme for the following two days was agreed. On arrival, both classes of English and Portuguese children sang songs to each other and climbed the hill together to the local church for brass rubbing and bell ringing and an exploration of the historic connections of the church, the school, the village and its setting. Following lunch in the school, the Lisbon pupils made preparations for the performance of their award winning processional march; the magnificent costumes and archways having been brought specially for the occasion. The afternoon ended with a presentation of a commemorative plate, a book of local scenes and a portfolio of pupils' work. In reply, Chris Truman was presented with the decorated archway used in the performance.

Links with Lisbon have been maintained through correspondence, and memories were revived when the school held a European week one year later. Pupils brought items of interest for a European exhibition and at the end of the week held a European activity afternoon involving staff from the feeder secondary school and parents. Included in pupil activities were Celtic design, cooking European foods and dishes, Scandinavian craft work, the programme of traditional regional dances and opportunities to speak in French and Norwegian.

At Christmas, the whole school held a European service in the Parish Church. This event involved pupils in the dramatisation of Baboushka, the singing of 'Silent Night' in German and performing a number of European folk dances including the Doubleska Polka from Yugoslavia. Three initiatives are planned for the current year. Spoken French will be developed on a regular basis with the Key Stage 2 pupils in co-operation with a colleague from the secondary school and all the area primary schools will be pursuing the European theme through song at the local music festival. Later in the year plans are underway to launch a small scale action research project on citizenship education with a small group of teacher researchers sharing a common interest in developing the European dimension.

Case history 2: researching Europe in action

Jean Gibson, deputy headteacher of a first school catering for pupils from a large 1930s suburban council estate adopted an action research approach to teaching about Europe with her year 3 class of seven to eight year-olds.

The main method of organisation was small group work within a cross-curricular thematic approach. Both group and class discussions were used as a means of enabling pupils to develop their own ideas and convey them to others. Children were involved in developing games and engaging in formal learning situations. Whenever appropriate, they were helped to use a variety of reference resources to discover information for themselves. This information could then be incorporated into the games designed by the pupils. She chose a geographical starting point 'Europe as part of the world'. This decision stemmed mainly from her previous experience of multi-racial teaching. In common with other infant teachers, she was unsure whether the use of maps was appropriate to the developmental level of the children. Her initial interest therefore focused on the children's present geographical knowledge, to see how far their understanding of maps, and countries, could be developed. She interviewed children and recorded class discussions to establish whether they had already developed concepts of the world in space and to determine the extent of their knowledge. Group discussions and other informal opportunities to explain what they were doing to others provided a check on the developing knowledge and understanding of the pupils. A teacher diary was kept, a photographic record was made and pupils' work was logged and stored for evaluation.

From the interviews and class discussions she established that:

● to use the children's interest in space as a starting point for the topic.
  purpose and could explain its shape,

- they appeared to understand the representation of land and sea on the globe and could differentiate between them,
- they knew the names of their home city and country, but had difficulty differentiating the two,
- they appeared not to know the word Europe,
- the interest level increased noticeably when the children were shown photographs relating to space,
- they appeared to understand the idea of photography from space and readily identified a purpose for satellite photography in the presentation of weather reports,
- they could identify several planets by their appearance,
- they could deduce 'cloud cover'.

Based on these findings, she decided:

- To use the children's interest in space as a starting point for the topic.
- to use the knowledge that the children already possessed re: the differentiation of land and sea, to develop the differentiation of the five main land areas (including Europe) – then, dependent on the level of interest and understanding, introduce the component countries of Europe,
- to avoid work requiring a knowledge of towns and cities.

With these principles in mind, she went on to develop seven related teaching activities.

Activity 1: the world from space

Using isomorphic photographs and slides of manned space flight, poster-sized satellite photos of earth, books about space, spacecraft and satellites, the children, either individually or in small groups, began to design and make their own space vehicles using junk materials. When these were completed and sprayed silver, they were hung from the ceiling around a large transparent globe.

Activity 2: Europe and the world

Using the large globe, the teacher and the pupils jointly devised games about the five main land areas.

A group would sit in a circle and roll the globe across to each other. The globe was stopped by the nearest pupil placing one hand on it, and the first person to identify the area of land nearest to the hand rolled the globe the next time.

Once the children were becoming familiar with the land shapes, a slightly harder game was devised. Two children would toss the globe to each other, catching it with two hands. They would then try to identify the location of both hands. A variation of this game allowed the child to look where one hand was, then try to work out where the other was likely to be.

Pupils quickly became proficient at these games, and were keen to take part. Several children began looking at the countries within the land areas, particularly where there was a distinctive shape, e.g. Italy quickly became a factor in identifying Europe. It now seemed appropriate to begin to focus the pupils' attention more closely onto Europe. At this stage, however, she had only used photographic material, and the globe as a representation of the earth. Some experience of flat maps and atlases seemed to be the next geographical step.

Activity 3: European countries – from globes to maps
Over the next week she looked at a variety of material and made her selections:

- using an atlas, the children looked down for the now familiar land shapes – in response to asking why an atlas might be used instead of a globe they readily suggested its more convenient, portable nature,
- the class then looked at a poster-sized satellite photograph of Europe, and looked at the shades of colour on the land – the pupils thought this was to do with things that grew there, and might be to do with how hot it was,
- the next step was to use a large plastic floor map of Europe – with no written information. This map showed boundaries. Children were able to suggest what these lines might be (from their earlier work with the globe) and understood that they were representational, therefore not on the photograph.
- next they considered the political map of Europe in the atlas. On this, the countries were all named and individually coloured. The class compared this to the photograph and the outline map. The children concluded that the colours were there 'to brighten it up' and 'to help us see where the countries are'. They readily understood that 'you can make it any colour you like when it's not a photograph – when someone has drawn it'.

At this stage the children began spontaneously to use the atlas alongside the outline map, to identify the countries, and made name labels. The labelling of the countries provided a basis for a game played either by two pupils, or two teams. The country names were distributed between them, and each took a turn at placing a name on a country. The use of the atlas was allowed. As their ability developed, the children devised a system of awarding points for correct placing challenging incorrect placing; time limits on looked up answers etc.

She later provided the children with A3 sized outline maps of Europe, so that individuals or groups could name and colour the countries. Planning their activity so that no two adjacent countries were the same colour interested them.

A few pupils asked for tracing paper and began to trace the map of Europe from the atlas. To provide an easier method for the children to draw their own maps, she set up an overhead projector with a transparency map of Europe. They drew round the outline which was projected onto paper fixed to the classroom wall. The teacher gridded one of the A3 maps and the children experimented with finding places from the grid reference. She then drew an equivalent grid (×9) on the back of a piece of vinyl floor covering. Using the grid reference squares, the pupils produced a floor map of Western Europe. They painted each country, but did not name them.

This floor map became the game board for a host of games. The most popular was a game similar to 'Twister', where, on the turn of a card, the child has to put his or her feet and hands on different, specified, countries. Another popular game was played by two teams. A pack of cards was used, each with a country name. As the card was turned, the first child to jump into that country won a point for his or her team. Colour cards were also used. As you jumped into a country painted that colour, you had to also give its name. Again, as the children became more proficient, the rules were developed and refined.

Activity 4: European flags
One of the atlases contained a chapter on flags. Several children had enjoyed looking for the flags of Europe, and had begun to draw them. This developed along the lines of the previous activity with country names. Games were then developed to include flags. Whilst the children had little difficulty with the name labelling games, the flags provided more of a challenge. The use of reference material was harder, because the flags were presented in alphabetical order, and not in a European section.

Activity 5: European currency
Coins from various European countries were put into the classroom for the children to handle and play with. In the course of this play, they began to sort the coins; usually by size or colour. She suggested that they might be used for the games on the maps. This produced an immediate difficulty. Although the children were keen, and a sufficient number had an adequate reading ability to make the exercise viable,

they found that they had to interpret what they read on the coin in order to place it on the map. They had encountered the languages of Europe in the country names on the coins. The children became interested in interpreting the country names, and finding the names of the currencies. Most offered language clues – but some e.g. Greece, were not obvious. Here they found the small European Community map that is produced by the European Commission, to be invaluable. It gives each country's name in its own language. So, the children quickly discovered that, by relating this map to the one in English, they could solve their problem.

At this point in the project, a competition for schools was advertised locally, with the focus being on Europe. If the children wanted their games to go into the competition, they would need to write out the rules. A written account would also need to accompany the collection of photographs of the developing project. Jean Gibson used this opportunity, while the children were highly motivated, to introduce them to the techniques of drafting to produce a good quality piece of finished work. The re-capping aspect of this work was useful in checking what had been understood, and could be explained by the children. The activity was completed by the Spring Bank Holiday, and was to have been the end of the project. However, soon after their return to school, they discovered that they were prize winners! The children's interest was immediately enlivened and led to a further extension of the activities.

Activity 6: European foods
During the local European awareness fortnight, the school meals service responded by providing menus with a European focus. The children discussed these in advance to see which foods were already familiar to them. They produced a map (using the O.H.P. method), and each day put the names of the foods on the country of origin. They also developed a histogram, of who had eaten what, and whether they had enjoyed it.

Activity 7: Europe of the twelve
Part of the prize was a set of balloons with the E.C. flag on them. The children had not encountered this flag before and were keen to know what it was and where it came from. The class researched this from Community produced materials. The children discussed the symbolism of the twelve stars, and reasons why a European Community might be a good idea. The main suggestions were 'So that

countries don't fall out', 'So you can share foods and things', 'To have the same sorts of rules'. Children began to use reference materials to discover more about the cultures of the countries, and they wrote about the things they found interesting. The work was illustrated by cut-outs from travel brochures. She found this the least satisfactory activity because of the quality of reference material available. The reference books and agency brochures tended to provide stereotyped information, that she felt was harmful to international understanding. As to future development, Jean Gibson considered that the interest in languages that occurred while the pupils were identifying coins was never developed. This could have been a starting point for language awareness work, using tapes, picture dictionaries, and popular story books that are produced in various languages.

Similarly, the attempt to study cultural aspects of the various countries, she thought, would improve in quality if European nationals were more closely involved – either in person, by visiting the school, or through international linking e.g. Campus 2000. Children would then, it was felt, be less dependent on stereotyped, and narrowly focused sources. Jean also felt that she needed to be more clearly aware of the connections with the National Curriclum programmes of study as these were (at that time) unfolding. She therefore engaged in a mapping exercise of the core subjects, English, mathematics and science at Key Stages 1 and 2 and submitted this analysis to the European dimension sub task group of the National Curriculum Council (see Appendix 4).

Case history 3: a view across a border

Louise Watson, teaching in the northernmost part of the U.K., is not subject to the legislation outlined in the Education Reform Act. She works within the provisions that apply specifically to Scotland. Her starting point was the commonly accepted maxim of good practice that children learn best when actively involved through personal experience within a structured framework.

In considering the place of Europe in her teaching she considered the most obvious approach was through environmental studies. She saw the main aim here as enabling children to extend their knowledge of themselves and the wider community in which they live, and equipping them with the skill necessary to make informed decisions. In this way, she outlined topics which she viewed as establishing the fundamental principles necessary to 'good citizenship' which she saw as closely related to 'European education'.

Consistent with her belief that developing European awareness should be continuous through the school, she mapped a progression of topics from the infant classes to top juniors:

(1) infants – myself, my home, my family, my friends,
(2) teeth – diet,
(3) Scotland,
(4) local study – E.C., enterprise.

In the infant classes, she stressed the importance of children learning not only about themselves but about other children and their families. She considered that by careful planning and skilful questioning, the teacher of this 'community' can lead children to explore and appreciate differences and form positive attitudes. Their personal experience of this community is gradually extended by inviting helpers into the classroom, e.g. parents, nurses, police, shopkeepers, etc. Thus the basic idea of interdependent relationships is formed by making full use of expertise within the school and its community.

Throughout the topic on 'teeth', children learn the importance of a healthy diet. By historic review, media focus and studying areas of deprivation, children expand their awareness of world-wide needs and begin to form opinions.

By progressing to a 'Vikings topic' at a later stage, an opportunity is afforded for an understanding of rules, place names, trade routes and the concept of invasion. These can all be linked with current issues and lead the child to explore and discuss his or her feelings/opinions, and identify the need for rules, trade, etc.

Louise Watson considered that once a 'healthy' awareness of others is developed in the curriculum, a detailed study of the home country can be made. Care is taken to foster proper and positive attitudes in relation to other people and countries. Informed comparisons may be encouraged but the need to appreciate others should be paramount. Increasing opportunities are then afforded, to consider cause and effect, and to debate the issues arising. Finally, in the age group nine to thirteen, opportunities grow for local study, making links with the E.C. and increasing enterprise awareness. Louise focused on exploring these possibilities by taking part in a pilot project on the teaching of languages other than English in the primary school. Her topic web of curricular activities is described in Appendix 5.

Case history 4: Europe around us in England

Sue Dennis is deputy headteacher of a rural primary school. The class she was teaching was comprised of 37, mixed ability, junior pupils aged nine to eleven years. Group work was the main teaching approach used to develop European awareness. She designed a small scale action research project identified through the following aims:

- to develop an interest and curiosity about the names and locations of individual countries, about rivers and mountain ranges, buildings, car signs, flags,
- to experience parts of the culture of the different countries so that the pupils could connect it with what they had learnt e.g. food, way of life, festival clothes, etc.,
- to accept differences as an interesting variety and think critically about clichés and prejudices,
- to promote breadth of experience, knowledge and understanding of the European dimension,
- to encourage the pupils to work co-operatively and collaboratively throughout the project,
- to provide opportunities for pupils to question, hypothesise, investigate and make judgements.

The following action research cycle (figure 3.2) indicates the methods used in evaluating the teaching/learning materials provided. The research questions to be addressed were:

(1) To what extent were the resources used?
(2) How were they used?
(3) What part did they play in the pupil's learning?

Action steps
Visit the local railway station
(links with towns, cities, counties, countries)

$\downarrow$

Ideas sheets to investigate the location of European countries and capitals

$\downarrow$

Dutch visitors
Brainstorming 'What do we already know about the Netherlands?
Use questionnaire 'What we would like to find out?'

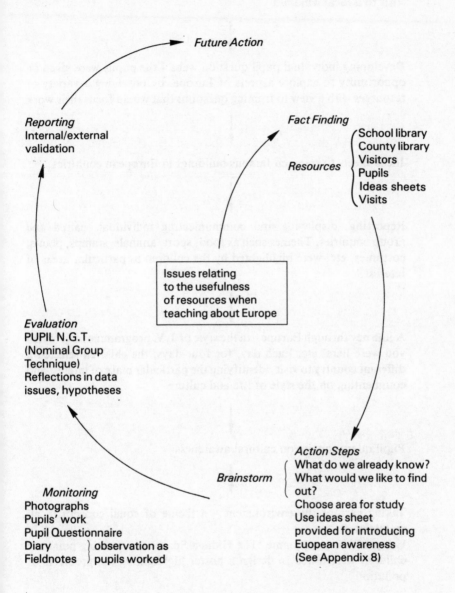

Figure 3.2   Action research cycle

Visit to a local windmill

↓

Developing individual pupil question webs – the pupils were given an opportunity to explore aspects of Europe, by providing a variety of resources with a view to framing questions that would focus their work

↓

Ideas sheets to research famous buildings in European countries

↓

Reporting, displaying and communicating individual, paired and group enquiries. Themes such as food, sport, animals, stamps, plants, costumes, etc. were highlighted by the children as particular areas of interest

↓

A journey through Europe – in the style of T.V. programmes e.g. 'Wish you were here' etc. Each day, for four days, the children selected a different country to visit, identifying the particular place of interest and commenting on the style of life and culture

↓

Pupil questionnaire on cultural awareness

↓

Taking care of the environment – a theme of equal concern to all countries
Using a T.V. programme 'The Hidden Spain' as a starting point the children were asked to design a poster highlighting the problems of pollution

↓

Links with Portugal
The pupils wrote a profile of themselves and their interests to send as an introductory pen pal letter to a group of Portuguese children

European elections
Role play to promote the pupils' ability to think critically

↓

Nominal Group Technique (O'Neil, 1981)
To evaluate the pupils' perceptions of the usefulness of the materials
provided to support their research

Resources
Local environment, visitors, pupils' experiences, county library
collection, school library, ideas sheets provided from Europe in the
primary school project, Post Office Euromap, Arnold jigsaw, map of
Europe, atlases, globes, artifacts, travel brochures, stamps, coins,
magazines, food labels, flags, newspapers, T.V. programmes, photographs, slides, postcards.

Evaluation
Sue Dennis analysed the data collected from implementing the action
steps and identified the following issues arising from the use of
resources in Teaching about Europe:

- it is important to begin with what the pupils already know, not only so
  that this may be built upon, but also so that any inaccurate information
  may be corrected,
- there should be some opportunity for the pupils to be involved in the
  planning of the project,
- the pupils should be encouraged to pose their own questions,
- pupils should be given scope for individual and group work,
- resources are a vital element of project work and pupils require time to
  become familiar with them in order to stimulate interest,
- it is not enough to provide and encourage a wide use of resources,
  pupils must be taught how to make effective use of them,
- pupils should be shown how to obtain information from pictures,
  photographs, diagrams, maps, etc.,
- pupils should have the opportunity to abstract information, to learn to
  argue rationally, and to take some responsibility for directing their
  own work,
- ideas sheets can be used successfully as aids to the pupils as well as to
  the teacher, extending individual and group work,
- if pupils are to benefit from this form of learning then the skills related
  to searching and using information i.e. extracting and summarising,
  note-taking, conveying ideas and constructing logical and sequential
  pieces of information need to be promoted,

- the pupils' evaluation (N.G.T.) indicated that human resources – visitors, were the most helpful and useful source of information for their research as there was immediacy of response, interaction and tangible similarities and differences.

Her concluding hypothesis for other teacher researchers to consider was, 'If children are to develop a positive attitude towards other countries and cultures then we must provide them with as many alternative resources as are necessary to create opportunities for learning and developing appropriate knowledge and skills'.

Case history 5: communicating with our European neighbours

Ken Round is deputy headteacher of one of the schools involved in the Doncaster European action research group described earlier. The school is situated in one of the many traditional mining villages with a mixed catchment area of private and council housing. There are 325 pupils on roll organised into 13 mixed ability classes according to age. Developing a European dimension was planned initially for one class of nine to ten year-olds. This approach was quickly extended to involve the whole year group – involving some 90 children, 3 class teachers, a member of the Teaching Support Service and a part-time teacher. He co-ordinated their work in close co-operation with the headteacher. From the outset, the teachers felt that the way forward was to explore possible ways of developing a European dimension in the existing philosophy of an integrated curriculum heavily based on first-hand experience.

In November 1989 the teachers were also beginning to implement National Curriculum science as the basis for their curriculum plan for that academic year. Bearing this in mind, they looked at the attainment targets for the programmes of study then available and devised a plan in which full use could be made of local opportunities to study European links. Their mapping of the National Curriculum for the Autumn Term 1989 and Spring Term 1990 is outlined in Appendix 6.

Under the umbrella title of 'Communications' they visited Doncaster railway station with the eventual aim of using this as a starting point for a journey to Europe. From this point, the three classes followed slightly different programmes of work; one class looked for evidence of European influence in the home and the village, another became involved in rail links and the Channel Tunnel, and the third produced a detailed analysis of questionnaire results and developed their reference skills. The year group teachers formulated their aims in four main areas of experience:

(1) To stimulate an awareness of, and an interest in, our European neighbours through the theme of Communication.
(2) To encourage the formation of positive attitudes towards people of different cultural and ethnic backgrounds.
(3) To foster the development of relevant geographical skills within the school's existing skills based learning programme.
(4) To plan, into subsequent topic work in school, a 'European dimension'.

The planning of the Communication topic had three distinct phases. The first phase involving the headteacher, topic work co-ordinator and Teaching Support Service, took place at a one day conference. Possible links between designated science attainment targets were identified and a broad outline plan of a progression of activities was drawn up.

The second phase involved the three teachers in the year group, one of whom was the topic co-ordinator, and the Support Service teacher who would be working closely with the three classes involved. At this stage the outline plan of activities was refined. Key ideas were identified, as were more specific links with National Curriculum attainment targets in science, maths, English and technology. Also at this stage modification of the suggested activities was considered as being appropriate to the needs of the children who were to be working with the Support Service teacher.

The third phase took place at an individual level with the teachers separately considering the proposed plan and devising their programme of study within this framework. This then became the working plan for that particular class for the duration of the topic. From this point each class initially followed a similar pattern but with activities organised in a variety of ways.

Throughout the period of the topic, activities were designed to achieve a balance between whole class, group and individual work along with opportunities for pupils to pursue their own chosen avenues of study. The three classes (4, 5, 6) proceeded to develop their own distinctive approach within this overall framework.

Class 4's work for the term centred round the theme of travel. In order to begin with their own experience they began with the question 'Which route do you take from home to school?' This work incorporated the use of large scale street maps of their village to encourage map reading skills and to emphasise a choice of route. The children were then involved in the construction of a simple questionnaire to be used on a visit to Doncaster railway station. Each child successfully interviewed one rail passenger. Back in school all the information was gathered together and entered onto a database.

The children used the globe and available atlases to locate Great Britain and to bring out the idea of it being an island. This led to considering travel outside Great Britain e.g. how to cross the water? – by sea and by air, later perhaps by using the Channel Tunnel. Why a Channel Tunnel and not a North Sea Tunnel? etc.

At this stage a historical aspect occurred to the teacher as he was reading the children's version of 'Around the World in Eighty Days' by Jules Verne; the emphasis being the use of steam engines for trains and ships – cars, planes etc. yet to be invented.

The class then moved onto the travel abroad theme with one child's Christmas visit to Australia compared/contrasted with other children's shorter journeys to European countries:

- travellers choose how to travel to their destination, making a sensible choice of route for them,
- is air travel appropriate – do they need the use of a car?
- package holidays – need to travel quickly,
- necessity of other forms of transport to/from airport,
- a closer look at Europe – use of atlases to identify countries and their capital cities, noting countries with and without sea borders,
- the development of study skills – how to use information books, gathering of facts,
- introduction of the idea that European products travelled to Great Britain, e.g. T-shirts from Portugal, fruits from France, Spain and Italy,
- recent developments in Eastern Europe provided opportunities for discussion e.g. the Berlin Wall, Romania – the supply of some engineering books donated by British engineers and the problems in transporting the books to Bucharest.

The use of a simple questionnaire involved the children in many different activities before, during and after the visit to Doncaster railway station. The teacher ensured the questionnaire was quick and easy to complete. Most passengers were intrigued and very cooperative. A good picture was built up of passengers' travelling preferences and this was easily transferred onto a database back in school.

In Class 5, the emphasis was on journeys. The summary plan was as follows:

Railways

(1) Visit to local railway station:

- children plan and devise a questionnaire for passengers which they test on each other, revise and print using a computer software package,
- visit Doncaster railway station. Tape-record tour around station. Interview passengers. Some children travel to Scunthorpe. Links with Europe noted, e.g. logo,
- on return to school, children analyse questionnaire in groups, putting data into 'Data Show' and determining reasons for responses and mapping results, e.g. destinations. Children also evaluate questionnaire.
  (M.A.T. 9, 12, 13, Sc.A.T. 12, E.A.T. 1, 2, 3, 4, G.A.T. 6).

(2) Visit local firm who design the drivers' cabs for the high speed trains to Europe:

- research newspaper articles in British Rail newspapers given on station visit for information about Europe and Channel Tunnel,
- visit; sit in driver's cab 'mock up' observe life size cab, talk to company director about design and implications of European rail link,
- map out locations in Europe made accessible by European rail link. Compare relative costings and travelling time,
- devise drama involving the first Channel Tunnel train journey for whole school assembly; involves Edinburgh link, stopping at Doncaster, European Women of the Year; social issues,
- use resource books from library service to find out about life in these European locations.
  (E.A.T. 1, 2, 3, G.A.T. 6, Sc.A.T. 5, M.A.T. 8).

(3) Design problem; packaging; design packaging to safely transport a chocolate egg by car to Kirn in Germany and return by post.

- plan package design, materials, weight, strength,
- make package, wrap and address in German,
- plan out route and estimate distance,
- receive package; evaluate, observe, calculate cost and time taken.
  (M.A.T. 8, 9, 10, E.A.T. 1, 3).

In Class 6, the class looked for examples of European influence in the home and the village.

(1) The children were asked to investigate their food cupboards at home and record from the packaging, the country of origin. Maps were then produced and the goods from various countries were listed and grouped.

(2)   A group investigated the cars on their street and classified these according to country of origin. Maps and bar charts were produced.

(3)   The class then investigated the cars in the school car park and grouped these according to country of origin. Use was made of 'Data Show' computer software to help illustrate results and findings.

(4)   (a) Half the class visited a local supermarket. A sixth former at a local comprehensive working in class on school experience provided a link here. Children had questions prepared, then in groups discovered products from Europe e.g. mode of travel, port of entry, route to shop etc.

      (b) The remaining half of the class visited a local motor company – an Alfa Romeo dealership. A previously prepared questionnaire for staff was used and the pupils discovered the country and city of origin and planned a route to the village. A history of Alfa Romeo was studied, who buys them, where customers live, and various aspects of technical information available from the model range was investigated.

At the end of the topic, the teachers evaluated their work and concluded that the scarcity and quality of resources available was a problem. This deficiency was turned to advantage in one class where the children and teacher plotted these shortcomings by questioning the accuracy of information from one book to another. It was judged that from the books made available that it was impossible to acquire a balanced view of Western Europe, let alone about Europe as a whole. The portrayal of stereotyping in the information provided affected the levels of awareness of other European cultures. The solution, it was felt, lay in setting up long term links with one or possibly two mainland European schools with whom the children could exchange experiences through videos, electronic mail, fax, pen correspondence, etc. The response of embassies and other agencies to letters sent by children greatly assisted motivation, especially when resources were provided such as maps, leaflets and brochures.

In future, the teachers recognised the need to start planning early, develop a bank of resources for common use, explore and maintain links with individuals or schools in other European countries and look afresh at local starting points for European awareness. The organisation of the project overall is outlined in Appendix 7.

The development of teaching and training materials

As we have seen, the scarcity (even in some cases the complete absence) of resources and well designed books suitable for a variety of ages and attainment levels encompassing all countries in Europe acts as a major constraint on the development of a European dimension in primary and middle schools. Work is underway on the idea of publishing materials that may be used in any classroom in Europe. While the realisation of this objective is a long term goal, some progress has been made. Starting from the school produced materials arising from the Reutlingen Action Research Unit work (Kasper *et al.*, 1990) a series of small scale teacher evaluation trials has been carried out in a second phase of the Europe in the Primary School project which began in 1987. Nine teacher evaluator groups were established in Spain (Madrid, Barcelona), Portugal (Lisbon), Holland (Amsterdam), U.K. (Sheffield, Humberside, Derbyshire), Italy (Milan, Catania) and Greece (Crete). The materials (150 sheets in total) sent to the evaluation groups were a draft version of a resource package which was later commercially produced in two edited forms (Kasper and Kullen, 1989; Koble and Kullen, 1990). A broad description of the ideas contained in the sheets is provided in Appendix 8.

It should be recalled that these ideas had their roots in action research amongst six schools in Western Germany in 1985 and were never intended to be adopted in other Member States. Similarly, several of the sheets distributed for evaluation were not available in full colour and/or suffered in quality in the reproduction process. With these considerations in mind, teacher evaluator groups produced reports over a six months trial period and their accounts were critically assessed by two colleagues who provided independent reviews of the evaluations provided. The outcomes give some tentative indications of the types of materials that might prove acceptable for multilateral use.

The following commentary draws upon the evaluation reports and assessor reviews with a view to offering some perspectives on in-house development of teaching and training materials and to assist the process of screening or selecting from existing resources.

The broadest measure of agreement on the suitability of the materials provided for evaluation centred on geographical/environmental aspects; e.g. teaching about physical features and the effects of civilisation on them. In dealing with cultural features, several of the groups stressed the importance of identifying and emphasising similarities in the context of differences. For example, the choice of visual images which portray contrasts should be carefully interpreted so as to avoid facile assumptions, say, about the distribution of wealth, the use of languages or ways of life. This can perhaps best be dealt with by providing a structured collection of resources that present a country in a multi-dimensional way. Examples of one dimensional stereotypes abound in tourist brochures; e.g. Ireland as the 'green island'; Holland as the 'land of tulips' etc. An important aspect of the European dimension will centre on demystifying stereotypes, perhaps most usefully in the context of media and communication studies. Thus, where images or concepts rely on a one-dimensional portrayal, these would be examined with a view to developing a critical understanding of their origins and functions. The portrayal is but one aspect of the problem of prejudice and how teaching can be structured so as to counteract the formation of unreflexive attitudes and unshakeable beliefs. Euro-centrism will, above all, need to be monitored against the criteria of a multi-cultural, multi-racial, multi-faceted community with interdependent relations with the rest of the world. Similarly, the richness and vitality of folk traditions from the past must not be allowed to obscure the dynamism and distinctiveness of modern ways of life in the countries concerned. In short, where comparisons are made they should be deconstructed in terms of their historical, economic and cultural origins.

The problems this approach raise, especially for the teaching of history, are too profound to be entered into here. But the general direction teachers of the European dimension may consider moving towards is well expressed by the team of Spanish teachers who suggest that colleagues should build up images of 'historical landscapes in time', just as they do with 'geographical landscapes in a space like Europe'.

Such an approach also offers a reminder of the limitations of resource based teaching. The tendency here may be to be too reliant on the materials made available at the expense of the reflection necessary for teachers to clarify their own knowledge, skills and attitudes towards a concept of Europe. In this connection, an action research approach provides an invaluable means of individual or team professional development. This appeal to the imaginative power of practitioners applies equally to pupils. They too need to be encouraged to hypothesise about their partners in Europe in an international framework to visualise, to suppose and to materialise ideas through actions and representations.

The evaluation of teaching and training resources will require the development of explicit criteria which suit local circumstances. The Dutch evaluation team for example adopted the following:

- the ability of the resource/information provided to reveal something worthwhile about people,

- the range of expressive/creative assignments stimulated,
- the opportunities provided for group discussion,
- the possibilities generated for active pupil response (play, drama, dance, song).

They considered that the most important design principles were:

- to secure an integrated multi-cultural approach,
- to reveal the political, social and economic relationships which exist between countries,
- to ensure the growth in pupil consciousness of the dependence which exists between countries,
- to provide topographic knowledge, especially concerning national and international structures,
- to raise levels of awareness of cultural diversity,
- to note the limits of factual knowledge and recognise experiential factors as central,
- to adopt a positive approach to European unity.

The adoption of these criteria will encourage pupils to develop a balanced experience of the European dimension in terms of knowledge, skills and attitudes. And because the underlying purpose is to support critical thinking, the teaching of controversial issues to do with, say, the central themes of the environment and cultural change will be tackled impartially.

But, the Dutch team warn against the tendency towards Europhoria and idealised internationalism, by failing to confront negative features of existing cultures and differences which have or may lead to conflict. For example: refugee problems, drug and alcohol abuse, migrant workers, religious differences, welfare levels, legal/judicial systems, etc. It would be unrealistic to expect that materials alone will solve the problem of teaching about such issues effectively, or indeed resolve concerns as to what level of attainment needs to be aimed for and at what stages of development. Nevertheless it must be faced squarely that the educative possibilities of the European dimension would be compromised if teaching materials restricted themselves to a surface awareness of issues or omitted to tackle uncomfortable realities from the past or the present.

Several of the outcomes reported from the E.C. teacher evaluator groups are echoed in a related evaluation study which arose in the Doncaster project described previously. The contribution made to the Doncaster project by the schools' librarian[5] arose from assembling books on all the countries of Europe with special emphasis on those countries in membership of the E.C. It was noted however that more fugitive material, e.g. audio-visual aids, posters, wallcharts etc. would have been desirable to collect especially when considering children with special educational needs. In line with H.M.I. recommendations, only material published within the last ten years were distributed. A total of 176 titles were made available for evaluation by the participating schools.

The results of this evaluation provide some pointers to good practice in policy development for selecting and supplying resources in support of the European dimension:

- coverage of individual countries was very patchy,
- there was nothing available for the primary age group on the theme of 'The Common Market',
- most material was weighted towards nine to ten years age range,
- there was a serious gap for infant or first schools and there was little suitable for older pupils with learning difficulties.

Most of the material was published in series format, e.g. 'Passport to' (Franklin Watts), 'Let's visit' (Burke), 'Focus on' (Hamish Hamilton). This leads to less diversity of approach than one would wish.

Despite choosing material published within the last ten years it was obvious that many recent developments were not covered. Most noticeable were the political changes in Eastern Europe. With the usual lead-in time for hardback published material it is unlikely that books which take this factor into account will appear in the immediate future. Opportunities, therefore, arise for teaching pupils a range of information skills, e.g. evaluating material by publication date, or choosing more appropriate material such as newspaper reports for very recent events.

The books available were not always well planned to encourage pupils to use the full range of information retrieval techniques, i.e. contents list, glossary, further reading list, index, etc. Equal opportunities issues were also highlighted. One teacher, for example, drew attention to the way many of the books portrayed the role of women, especially through the choice of illustrations and photographs. Very few books showed the ethnic diversity present in many European countries. The pupils seemed to prefer the very straightforward, factual approach, presumably for ease of reference. Books with a more narrative style, e.g. describing the daily life of a typical child or family, were not as popular.

The English National Curriculum reading attainment target level (i.e. pupils aged fourteen years) asks pupils to 'recognise, in discussion, whether subject matter in non-literary and media texts is presented as fact or opinion'. This has implications for nine to thirteen year-old middle schools in particular. In addition it has implications for the way non-narrative text is presented by authors and publishers.

One area which was found to be particularly difficult to resource was the choice of suitable fiction texts with a 'European cultural dimension'. The publishing market is an international one with many co-productions, especially of picture books. However, this leads to a reduction in differentiation with what is sometimes referred to as the 'Eurobook approach' rather than retaining the essential character-istics of the country of origin. Often novels lose something in trans-lation and the general impression gained was that there were very few European mainland authors whose books were enjoyed by young readers in the schools surveyed. Visits made by school library service staff to individual schools indicated that much of the stock in those primary and middle schools contacted dated from the 1960s or, at best, the mid-70s.

The need for schools to update their book stocks to take into account the European dimension has not gone unrecognised but the cost implications for schools are disturbing. For example the price of the highly regarded 'Passport to' series, (Franklin Watts) is considered high in the context of schools struggling to resource the National Curriculum core subjects effectively. Local management of schools is not likely to make that struggle any easier, indeed it may make matters worse, for example by reducing the amount of resources assistance the school library service can give.

The main conclusion of this evaluation seemed to be that there are very few books or series which can be recommended without any reservations. Better picture/poster resources are urgently required especially for the early years. Such fugitive material is difficult for teachers to trace. The recently published 'Resources for Teaching About Europe' (Central Bureau, 1990) may assist in meeting this need.

Whatever is ultimately provided by publishers, whether print-based or not, it was judged that unless schools received additional resources they would not be equipped to tackle the challenges and opportunities of 1992. The suggestion was made that perhaps the E.C. should launch a teaching materials purchase scheme for this purpose.

The scarcity of teaching materials is mirrored by the restricted availability of tailored training materials. Two interesting examples may however serve to illustrate the linkage between the need to develop teaching and resource materials and the need to promote training.

The first example from Sheffield arose from a small project grant from the Central Bureau supported by Sheffield L.E.A.[6] The aim of the project was to encourage and support in-service teacher education in the European dimension. The draft materials to emerge for trial consisted of seven modules which were designed to cater for teachers in both primary and secondary schools and could be used singly or together. The first trial module was intended to encourage a group of teachers to draw upon each other's backgrounds, specialities, interests and experiences so that the group's understanding of the European dimension could be enriched.

The second module aimed to raise awareness of the European dimension by focusing on seven related themes: what is Europe?; destroying stereotypes; interdependence; communication and language awareness; National Curriculum; human rights; and current European issues. The third module aimed to maximise opportunities for making direct contacts with other European children. The intention was to encourage first-hand experience of other cultures through electronic or more conventional means. It also helped to create networks by informing teachers of existing contacts and links. For example, in Sheffield the module disseminated the work of the 'Friends Around the World' project which aimed to link Sheffield pupils in friendship with children in other parts of the world and other regions of the British Isles. It also gave some useful advice and a check list on the organisation of study visits and exchanges. Module 4 focused on the primary school and provided an opportunity to review resources and consider ideas for Teaching about Europe based upon geographical knowledge, common cultural aspects, places in Europe, travel, landscape and environment, aspects of Europe within the British Isles, European history and economic and industrial factors.

The fifth module was structured to cater for the interests of secondary schools based upon three main approaches; a linked series of single periods, a suspended timetable and integration into broad curriculum areas. Module six provided an opportunity to consider the European dimension as part of a whole school policy and module seven offered a model for evaluating courses of training on the European dimension.

The second example from Nottingham Polytechnic's Centre for European Education (Antonouris, 1990) provides materials for use in both initial and in-service teacher training. The materials take the form of two activity books. The first book is structured by means of an inter-cultural European perspective and adopts a specific approach to the management of topic and project work. Themes such as: 'Minorities and Languages, Working in Another Country, Personal Names and Place Names', aim to develop understanding of ethnic and cultural diversity and confront stereotyping, prejudice, racism and sexism. Activity Book 2 extends discussion of issues to the National Curriculum and environmental concerns. In common with Book 1, it also provides examples of cross-curricular themes and ideas for evaluating pupil's work at both primary and secondary level.

This particular approach taken to the European dimension extends the work of Antonouris and Wilson (1989). The inter-cultural perspective presented is based upon eight main principles; European diversity focusing on the many inter-related cultural communities to be found, global diversity expressing achievements and contributions towards world development from many continents, regional focal points as exemplifying a European migratory society, common experience stressing similar needs, positive images portraying achievements of a variety of cultures and peoples from both Europe and the rest of the world, anti-racist strategies actively combating prejudice, and anti-sexist action in a context where the school itself is experienced as 'an equal opportunities zone'.

The complementary rationale to this perspective derives from Wilson's work on the management of topic work. This approach asks of teachers that they determine what knowledge they consider to be essential as an outcome of the experience of any given topic and how this will develop pupils' ability to think in an analytical and critical way. He proposes that access to the European dimension as in any topic/thematic approach, can be made through identifying the main ideas and related concepts. Thus, the main ideas of the European environment, group behaviour and change would provide worthwhile knowledge for pupils to acquire. By adopting a 'ladder of thinking' about an idea or concept, tasks can be set that require pupils to:

● identify and describe the idea,
● undertake appropriate classifications,
● compare, seek similarities and differences,
● suggest causes, look for reasons,
● predict and explain consequences and effects,
● make judgements about and give opinions on,
● apply the knowledge gained to new situations and make generalisations. (Antonouris and Wilson 1989: 25)

While some selection will need to be made in individual cases, teaching and learning activities generated from this hierarchy will ensure that pupils acquire skills and develop concepts that can also be applied to other topics and fields of knowledge.

Conclusions

A variety of approaches can be traced in order to develop a European dimension, but whatever the selection made they should have an explicit rationale that will address not only the question of knowing about Europe but also the experience of being a European in a multi-cultural society. The dangers of Euro-centrism are properly checked by a full recognition that the European dimension is on the one hand a contribution to the whole curriculum and on the other an essential component of the larger and more important goal of international understanding. A conceptual map of the dimension I have proposed will minimally include teaching and learning activities concerned with developing personal and national identity, education for the global environment, inter-cultural understanding, citizenship and economic and industrial understanding.

At the heart of the process of developing a European dimension of the curriculum is a condition common to the general enterprise of educating pupils, i.e. a commitment to worthwhile knowledge and understanding in depth and breadth, and the capacity to discriminate between intrinsic and instrumental values. This will require both a thinking pupil and a thinking school. The temptation to avoid contro-versial issues and conflicting values can be tackled not only through ensuring the adoption of teaching styles which emphasise critical reasoning, but also by taking personal and social education as seriously as the core subjects.

The new dimension among the many new dimensions of the National Curriculum will be a revitalised consideration of citizenship education for children in primary and middle schools. All of this will require the development of policies in the framework of whole school planning. The participation necessary to bring this about will be an essential ingredient in the management of change. The following chapter is concerned with exploring some implications of adopting this strategy.

CHAPTER 4

School Development for a Common Educational Community

Development planning has been an essential tool in industry and commerce for many years. While teachers have always planned their lessons, and groups of teachers have frequently engaged in developing schemes of work, an integrated approach to the management of change has not always been a feature of school organisation. This situation can partly be explained by a tradition of teacher autonomy which the Education Reform Act in 1988 has radically transformed. Indeed, the main innovation of the Act may be judged to be fore-closure on a well established tradition of teacher based development and accountability being switched to organisation development instead. Curriculum implementation rather than curriculum development, and school management rather than class management are now the main post Reform Act requirements.

The National Curriculum Council's commitment to the 'whole curriculum' provides a crucial interpretation of the way in which these reforms are to be understood. Such a perspective clearly signals that not everything a pupil needs to know can be satisfactorily expressed in terms of core and foundation subjects. The cross curricular elements such as problem-solving, personal and social development and study skills including the uses of information technology are highlighted; themes such as economic and industrial understanding, careers and guidance, health, citizenship and environmental education are emphasised together with dimensions such as equal opportunities and preparing pupils for 'life in a multicultural, multilingual Europe which, in its turn is interdependent with the rest of the world' (N.C.C. 1990a: 3). The scale of such a programme readily illustrates the need

111

for a reliable means of controlling the information overload and innovation saturation which arises. Moreover, the smaller the school the longer the timescales that will be needed for such changes as are necessary to be introduced. The single overriding strategy therefore in managing for change in such circumstances must be school development planning.

School development planning

While it has recently become a requirement of the Department of Education and Science that all Local Education Authorities receive annual development plans from their schools, not every school has grasped the significance of this requirement as a means of securing an insurance policy against unreasonable expectations or for controlling the scope, pace and focus of change efforts.[1]

There are at least five main reasons why a planning approach to developing a European dimension is necessary.

(1) It provides an up-to-date statement of the role and identity of the school. While every school claims to have distinctive if not unique aims and needs, a statement in the form of a development plan justifies such claims and clarifies individual purposes.

(2) A review of policies is regularly carried out recognising that effective management arises when policies are established and modified in the light of experience.

(3) Operational rules are made explicit in order to clarify and implement policies. To work effectively, such policies are planned to match circumstances on timescales that create opportunities and meet needs.

(4) Monitoring and evaluating, with a view to improvement of initiatives taken, are built into the management practices of the school. In this way, objectives are assessed for appropriateness and effectiveness.

(5) Aims and intentions are recorded and documented within consciously selected boundaries. In this way, benchmarks are established for later appraisal of performance.

Such principles can be summarised in the following form:

Planning processes

translate
PURPOSES
into
POLICIES
into

PLANS
to ensure
IMPLEMENTATION
FEEDBACK
and
REVIEW

In essence, a planning approach to developing a European dimension is a search for clarity in terms of mission, process and procedures. Its principles are illustrated in figure 4.1 below.

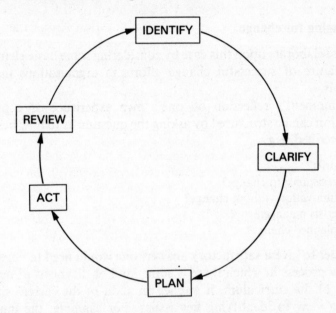

Figure 4.1

It is crucial to recognise the importance of timescales in the management of change. This implies that there are different types of development plans that need to be made in support of the European dimension:

- a *strategic plan* setting long term aims over a period of three to five years,
- a *medium term development plan* outlining the main objectives to be achieved over two to four years,
- a *short term action plan* identifying immediate tasks, targets and strategies to be achieved by designated individuals with specific responsibilities for key issues.

In summary, I believe that in the current climate, a European dimension of the curriculum will not emerge without an effective planning regime for a number of reasons, not least of which is the recognition that it may be perceived to be a controversial issue either because it threatens other possibilities or is considered to be a low priority. Either way, and on account of the fact that it will confer wider benefits on the school, a school development planning approach must be considered to be a pre-condition for effectively developing a European dimension.

Managing for change

Let me elaborate upon this case by considering some basic elements of the nature of successful change efforts in organisations including schools.

A moment's reflection on one's own experience of a practical situation can be structured by asking the question as to how best it can be described, e.g.

- drift?
- resistance to change?
- innovation without change?
- crisis management?
- planned change?

In order to give a satisfactory answer, one would need to engage in a review process in which there is some kind of diagnosis of needs. In terms of the curriculum, it implies an audit of the current situation with a view to identifying key issues. For example, the impact of programmes of study on core subjects; assessment procedures to ensure continuity, transition between phases and effective moderation; the managment of topic and project work; record keeping; and the management arrangements necessary to meet the specific educational needs of pupils. Not least of these concerns for our purpose is the management of cross curricular elements. This will require the development of whole school and cross phase policies which in view of the limited resources available must imply careful selection of priorities.

The identification of needs and development priorities can be structured more or less formally and more or less collaboratively. One of the ways of achieving structured fact finding is to adopt the G.R.I.D.S. system.[2] Such preliminaries to effective development of a European dimension can be further strengthened by considering the three main change tasks that participants in a change effort will need to address:

- introducing new or revised materials,
- developing new skills and related teaching styles,
- encouraging modification to attitudes and beliefs.

Each of these tasks will require a variety of means to implement them effectively. The conditions under which successful innovation occurs has been well described by Fullan (1986) who carried out a review of research on the implementation of educational change. Among the factors he identifies for improving implementation are the following:

(1) In educational settings, overload is inevitable, therefore, one must select a few important changes, but implement these very well.
(2) Attention to detail is crucially necessary to successful change efforts and is usually neglected.
(3) Using what is already known about the process of organisational change and the content of the curriculum development desired is an essential ingredient to success in implementing change. Moreover one must implement the plan, hence the central importance of action planning.
(4) Change essentially means adults learning. Developing practice must therefore entail teachers becoming learners in their own classrooms.

Finally, a comment is made which provides a fitting summary to any consideration of the management of change, 'Effective change, even if voluntarily pursued, rarely happens unless there is pressure and support.'

Recalling that the sense of 'community' to which I drew attention requires both collaboration and participation, it is critical to recognise that the underpinning necessary to whole school development planning is founded upon the organisation of consent. Handy (1977) in his influential book on understanding organisations outlines six management principles that maximise this condition:

- recognising the right to disagree,
- controlling by planning not checking,
- managing by reciprocal trust,
- creating task groups,
- encouraging personal styles,
- husbanding energies.

The organisation of consent begins by the articulation of policies. The leader of a change effort whether as headteacher, deputy or curriculum co-ordinator, will see the need for a statement of policy to give a clear sense of direction for the initiatives that follow from it. This strategy is consistent with Lewin's (1964) graphic outline of effective change processes in terms of cycles of 'unfreezing', 'moving' and 're-freezing'. Policy making helps to unfreeze; development planning gets the school moving in desired directions; and action planning re-freezes in a way that gives participants a clear sense of purpose within a framework of defined objectives.

Bearing in mind that effective change requires both pressure and support, a variety of strategies must be employed. Bennis (1976) describes these as falling under three main categories:

- 'power–co-ercive' in which the exercise of authority compels certain activities to be carried out,
- 'rational–empirical' in which persuasion and the offering of evidence is used as a means of getting things done,
- 'normative–re-educative' whereby involvement in structured situations alters attitudes and beliefs through direct engagement with alternative norms and values.

Such strategies are linked with certain styles of organisation. Macdonald (1977) has described these in terms of autocratic, bureaucratic and democratic modes. A more recent style which combines one or more of these has been termed 'managerialist' (Ball, 1990).

The effective developer of the European dimension will see that managing consent will mean orchestrating these various approaches and will for example seek to combine in the creation of task groups three main types of participants;

- the *change agent*, able to intervene in situations with a view to improving the organisation of teaching and learning,
- the *support agent*, capable of involving people and well versed in both the specifics of curriculum content and the processes of curriculum development and
- the *link agent*, skilled in facilitating contacts and able to supply resources and effectively disseminate the outcomes of evaluated experience.

Above all, the adoption of a development planning approach will recognise a distinction between rational planning and action planning. Too often, elaborate plans are laid as if these alone were sufficient to ensure success. They must be accompanied by implementation measures through which planning is translated into practice; in short, the activity of planning does not ensure action.[3]

Action planning

While the processes of school development planning have recently been outlined (D.E.S., 1989), the underlying processes that ensure implementation have been less well described. The following section takes the form of a proposed format for an action plan. It is intended to be used as a component part of the school development plan and aims to structure the efforts of task groups established to pursue the priorities identified through a survey of opinion and diagnosis of needs. It is suggested that an essential accompaniment to this framework is headteachers, deputies or curriculum co-ordinators liaising with task groups over one or more ten-week blocks leaving weeks at the beginning and end of each term for preparation and reporting.

Action plan for developing a European dimension

Area for development
List here topic/work/task/policy/priority for development.
Purpose: to clarify direction of change.

Name of co-ordinator
Nominate main person with delegated responsibility to develop, implement and arrange for the evaluation of the plan.
Purpose: to focus leadership and facilitate support.

Task group(s)
Name of main persons with responsibility for implementing the plan. Ideally, the group should include an external facilitator and/or evaluator.
Purpose: to delegate functions, increase internal communications, help dialogue.

Statement
A very brief outline of the group's mission – what it is created to achieve. This should be written for an external audience of parents, governors, advisers, as much as for members of the school staff.
Purpose: to assist external communications and help to clarify tasks amongst participants.

Roles

Identify responsibilities and terms of reference for the co-ordinator and each group member.

Purpose: to avoid conflict, specify intentions and clarify expectations.

Analysis of needs

Conduct a critical examination of the strengths, weaknesses, opportunities and threats posed to the school in the area for development.

Purpose: to demonstrate that a diagnosis of needs has been carried out and to provide a benchmark for a summative (final) evaluation.

Strengths: outline what is currently done well.

Weaknesses: identify where development work needs to be carried out.

Opportunities: locate the possibilities for growth in the situation being studied.

Threats: anticipate problems, barriers and potential difficulties.

Strategies

Having predicted areas of resistance to change, describe in general terms how each of the following change tasks are to be tackled:

(a) introducing new or revised materials;
(b) supporting the adoption of new skills or modifying teaching styles;
(c) encouraging changes in attitudes or beliefs.

Objectives

List the main objectives to be achieved in priorty order as these relate directly to the longer time scale of the school development plan. A calendar of specific dates should be drawn up to relate both the strategies and the objectives to a practical scheme for managing them over one or more ten week blocks.

Action steps

List the main action steps, in priority order, to be taken over the block of time chosen.

Purpose: to further clarify intentions, to communicate them and prepare both support and resources.

Evaluation

Identify the criteria to be used to confirm the successful achievement of the action steps. These are often very difficult to describe, but are essential to make clear; from the most trivial and obvious improvements to the more subtle and complex.

Purpose: enabling assessment of performance.

Fact finding
Identify the main sources of information to be drawn upon ranging from published studies, through the experience of fellow practitioners, to the advice of external advisers etc.
Purpose: to improve the quality of decision making to avoid re-discovering what is already well accepted, to inform the diagnosis of needs and to clarify action steps and performance indicators.

Diagnosis of the situation
Identify self or group evaluation procedures to be used with the staff on a whole school basis, e.g. N.G.T., G.R.I.D.S. or D.I.O.N.[4]
Purpose: to assist in refining action steps, gaining consensus and providing a critical overview.

Monitoring
Specify what kinds of data are to be collected on the implementation of action steps.
Purpose: to assist in evaluating action as this evolves.
Media for data collection can include:
> pupils' work
> photographs
> audio-tape
> video-tape

Critical appraisal
What arrangements are to be made for internal and external evaluation?
Internal evaluation: What procedures are to be followed in cross-comparing data sets? How is the group to compare outcomes? When?
External evaluation: What arrangements have been made to involve outsiders to assist in validation plans and reports in an effort to promote objectivity? When?

Reporting
Identify the type of report to be made at chosen intervals, specify the audience and indicate the mechanisms to be used for feedback/review; how, when, where? A suggested structure is based on three types of report:

Feasibility (end of term one)
Preferably entirely restricted to the Task Group and head-teacher/deputy – two to three pages.

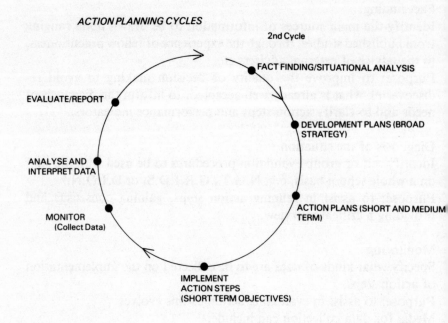

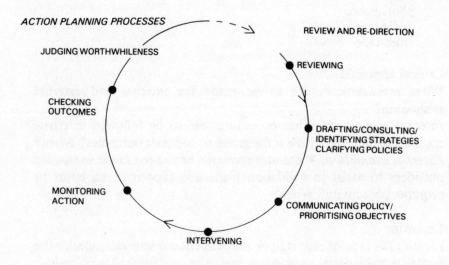

Figure 4.2 Action planning cycles and processes

Progress (end of term two)
Having a wider circulation to staff/governing body and to an external review panel/assessor/evaluator – five to ten pages.
Final (end of term three)
Addressed to the staff and governing body it should be structured to match the action plan with recommendations. It should contain an appendix which outlines the action plan for the next cycle of development, linked to the review of the school development plan.

The processes which underline the action planning framework have a close resemblance to the processes of action research that were adopted by the Europe in the primary school project (see figure 4.2).

Developing practical professional knowledge

The increasing tendency to relate professional development opportunities to school based activities is a welcome evolution in the design of in-service training. The further possibility of an award bearing outcome for advanced study is an additional benefit in building a knowledge base of good practice. For if we are to succeed in progressively building a partnership with our European neighbours through closer co-operation, there must evolve a tradition of what I referred to earlier as inter-cultural pedagogy. The central aim is a relatively simple one, translating the theory of a common market into the practice of educational institutions. In recognition of the formidable philosophical and cultural obstacles to achieving this aim, there is a clear need for more and better supported efforts to encourage research based teaching on the European dimension. I shall not attempt to dwell on the rationale of this case as I have argued it extensively elsewhere (Bell, 1985, 1988). My main purpose here is to suggest that developing a European dimension in the educational programmes of primary and middle schools needs to proceed at a number of levels. I have so far expressed these as consisting of:

(1) A statement of policy, collaboratively developed in full consultation with pupils, parents, teachers, advisers, governing bodies and external agencies.
(2) Locating a policy statement within the framework of a school development plan in which a survey of opinion and diagnosis of needs leads to the selection of priorities for action.
(3) Developing an action plan to structure implementation of policies and priorities, to involve task groups, and develop targets set out over an achievable timescale.

From this baseline, I suggest that:

(4)   By increasing the rigour and scope of the data collection methods used to monitor action, and by submitting the stages of implementing the action plan to various forms of validation, a secure foundation for research based teaching is provided.

Data collection can be selected from the following sources:

- finding out from published studies what is said about the action proposed,
- surveying field experience (contacts amongst colleagues),
- teacher diaries/logs of events,
- pupil diaries/logs of events,
- interviews,
- observations,
- questionnaires,
- review panel/external assessor/adviser commentary,
- group evaluation procedures,
- self evaluation check lists,
- testing.

The increasing availability of external agencies able to offer accreditation for school-based activities of this type in part fulfilment of an external award represents an important means of linking staff development policies with the European dimension. Steps are already being taken by a number of higher education institutions to develop joint Masters degrees with European partners within a framework of co-operation based upon action inquiry. This opens up the future possibility of the exchange of teachers and part-time study leading to a higher degree. By 'action inquiry' I mean a strategic relationship between an investigation involving direct intervention in a practical situation with a view to improvement (action research) and a non-intervention investigation structured so as to improve judgement on the types of action that would make improvements to practice most likely (case study). Thus:

(5)   A further stage of development beyond research based teaching is the adoption of an action inquiry approach. This approach is outlined in figure 4.3 below.

Finally, a combination of elements 1–5 leads naturally to a final stage.

(6)   The launching of a whole school action inquiry project on the European dimension in which collaborative school improvement is the chief aim. The management of such projects is outlined in figure 4.4 below.

ACTION RESEARCH

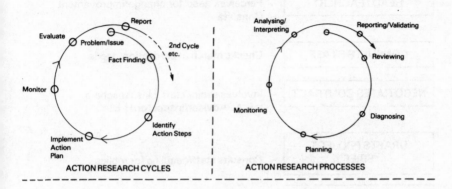

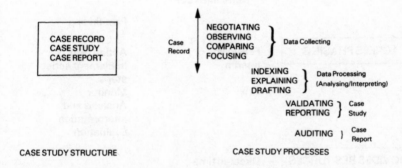

Figure 4.3 Structure and processes of action inquiry

The experience of adopting a whole school action inquiry project has been fully described elsewhere (Bell and Colbeck, 1989). As the major implications of the Reform Act work their way through schools, it may prove increasingly possible to adopt such an approach for it serves to bring together a number of factors that are known to influence the quality of teaching and learning including co-operation between various partners, bridging gaps between theory and practice, using the products of educational research to improve decision making, supporting effective leadership, and developing knowledge of practice through broadening the base of participation in policy making. Above all, the procedures are designed to encourage critical reflection on practical problems arising within a school and are aimed at providing a systematic means of testing proposed improvements.

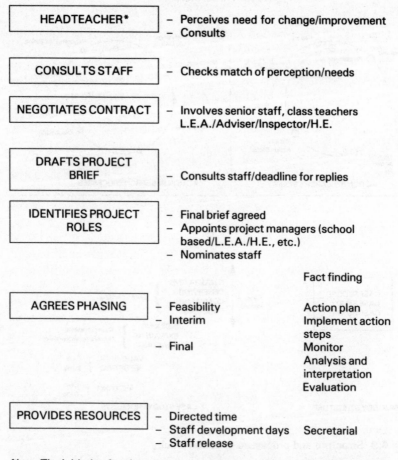

| HEADTEACHER* | – Perceives need for change/improvement |
| | – Consults |

| CONSULTS STAFF | – Checks match of perception/needs |

| NEGOTIATES CONTRACT | – Involves senior staff, class teachers L.E.A./Adviser/Inspector/H.E. |

| DRAFTS PROJECT BRIEF | – Consults staff/deadline for replies |

| IDENTIFIES PROJECT ROLES | – Final brief agreed
– Appoints project managers (school based/L.E.A./H.E., etc.)
– Nominates staff |

Fact finding

| AGREES PHASING | – Feasibility   Action plan
– Interim   Implement action steps
– Final   Monitor
   Analysis and interpretation
   Evaluation |

| PROVIDES RESOURCES | – Directed time
– Staff development days   Secretarial
– Staff release |

Note: The initiative for change may come from a variety of sources both internal and external. The various steps described could profitably be delegated to emphasise the necessity of collaboration and ownership. Nevertheless, the formal decision making described must be taken by the headteacher in conjunction with the governing body.

Figure 4.4 Outline project management strategy

In order for the interests of all participants to be protected as far as it is reasonably possible, it will be necessary to adopt a code of conduct for the purpose of action inquiry. This may be particularly important in the context of international/inter-cultural collaboration. A suggested outline is given below:

(3) Have roles and responsibilities been clearly specified?
(4) To what extent is the analysis of needs underpinned by data collected within the school?
(5) How far have the priorities identified been informed by information including research findings, local and national reports, and advice from experienced practitioners, advisers and others beyond the school?
(6) What evidence is there to assume that the objectives and their ranking have been agreed in consultation with colleagues?
(7) Does each one of the stated objectives meet the following test:

- has identified specific outcomes,
- is measurable in one or all of its aspects,
- is achievable,
- is relevant,
- is time related.

(8) Are the action steps able to address one or more of the following:

- introducing new or revised materials,
- supporting the adoption of new skills or modified teaching styles,
- encouraging changes in attitudes or beliefs.

(9) Are the evaluation criteria clear?
(10) How is this plan to be evaluated?
(11) Is the action plan convincingly embedded in an annual cycle of school development planning?
(12) Have the necessary resources for support been acknowledged and supplied?

By adopting procedures such as those described, a systematic attempt will be made to manage a situation characterised by innovation saturation. This will also have the benefit of linking the European dimension clearly to the context of whole school development planning. It will also recognise the fact that cross-curricular dimensions and issues are some of the most difficult aspects of the curriculum to implement effectively. In an international review of multi-cultural, educational programmes (C.E.R.I., 1989), the bleak fact is confronted that many such programmes are relatively ineffective. The report argues that in-depth consideration must be given to what is involved in the transmission of culture within the school. I suggest that an action planning approach will provide this opportunity. Moreover, by linking action planning to a whole school development plan, the future prospect of appraisal can be logically and supportively linked and be focused on job satisfaction as distinct from performance deficiencies. However, the first step in developing a

European dimension must be a review of the existing curriculum followed by an evaluation of its present status *vis-à-vis* Europe. This can then be followed by a development planning approach as I have outlined. Some reflections on the broader aspects of such a curriculum in action is explored as a concluding theme.

CHAPTER 5

A Curriculum for Europe in Action

> Animals are divided into; (a) belonging to the Emperor, (b) embalmed, (c) tame, (d) sucking pigs, (e) sirens, (f) fabulous, (g) stray dogs, (h) included in the present classification, (i) frenzied, (j) innumerable, (k) drawn with a very fine camel hair brush, (l) etcetera, (m) having just broken the water pitcher, (n) that from a long way off look like flies. (Source: Ancient Chinese Encyclopaedia). In the wonderment of this taxonomy, the thing we apprehend is one great leap, the thing that, by means of fable, is demonstrated as the exotic charm of another system of thought, is the limitation of our own, the stark impossibility of thinking *that* but what is it impossible to think, and what kind of impossibility are we faced with here? (Foucault, 1970)

The prospect of a Europe without economic frontiers has implications for a union without cultural or educational barriers too. Will this mean a Euro-curriculum?

In one sense, this hardly matters if the principles explored in the foregoing chapters are to be accepted, refined and themselves critically examined in the light of experience. In any event it is hardly unthinkable for, despite its mayfly existence, the U.K. has already had in recent times experience of union with another European mainland country for example when, on 16th June 1940, Churchill and De Gaulle formally stated 'The two Governments declare that France and Great Britain shall no longer be two nations but one Franco-British Union. The constitution of the union will provide for joint organisation of defence, foreign, financial and economic policies.'[1] So, the issue of national sovereignty, frequently the subject of intense debate, takes on a quite different hue when viewed against the lessons of modern history.

The standpoint taken by Jean Monnet, who played such a vital role in the creation of a European community, was that the concept of sovereignty was outmoded where national institutions prevented a coherent approach to interests held in common such as world trade, monetary affairs and security. The intention of a common European community was in his view to complement rather than rival such institutions. His preferred method was based upon organisation, and organisation directed towards the common interest. Determining this common interest depended on the drawing up of a 'balance sheet' which accounted for the resources available and the constraints to be observed (Kohnstamm, 1981). In the aftermath of the Reform Act, the constraints on developing a European dimension are severe and the resources strictly limited. A balance sheet is clearly necessary.

But the tendencies towards cultural degeneration from self-absorption and the pre-occupations of the immediate can be counter-balanced by considering the whole problem of educating children for a world in which the four freedoms of an economic community: freedom of movement for goods, services, capital and people is shortly to be achieved among 320 million adults including 70 million pupils. It seems inconceivable that in this context, the fifth freedom of educational ideas – will be finally denied.

It might also be recalled that the central issue of identity, supposedly enshrined in national education systems, is a construction of modern times (Grant, 1973). Similarly French and German speaking English kings are not so far distant from the British experience either. National identity is but one possibility. For the imagination, once empowered to recognise and experience alternatives, is enabled to contemplate choices without contradictions and undertake roles without necessarily renouncing roots. This effect can be seen in the various action programmes approved under the terms of European education policy as this has evolved. For such actions have had an important 'knowledge sharing' influence (Neave, 1984). Co-operation in these circumstances has meant that a contribution has been made to national policies through learning from the experience of partners. The confidence engendered through this approach may indeed lead to removal of educational frontiers.

The official view of this possibility has, paradoxically, all the appearance of sanguine acceptance – judging from the responses made by the twelve Members States to a recent Commission questionnaire on incorporating a European dimension in education. However, Ryba's (1989) analysis of this exercise is that there is a dysfunction between official viewpoints and the alternative views of expert commentators who see less room for satisfaction, particularly on the pace of progress and the appropriateness of published materials. So the problem of achieving effective educational co-operation is compounded not only by existing constitutional barriers, but also perceptions of achieving their removal or even the necessity of modifying them. Such circumstances suggest the existence of attitudes and beliefs which have deeper roots.

McLean (1990) in examining these issues and the prospects for a common school curriculum which would include Britain, identifies the way school knowledge traditions are regarded in the different countries of the existing Community as the most serious obstacle. He suggests there are three main competing ideologies; Encyclopaedism based upon universality, rationality and utility; Humanism centring upon morality, individualism and specialism; and Naturalism based upon philosophical, psychological and sociological evidence on the way human beings develop towards mental and physical maturity.

His comparative analysis of the distribution of these ideologies and their embedding in national educational systems yields the conclusion that 'rational thinking is not encouraged in English educational objectives to the extent that occurs in the majority of European countries' (McLean, 1990: 117). Moreover, he judges that the effectiveness of alternatives on this criterion places, 'English youth at a serious disadvantage compared to their counterparts in other countries in the labour market.'

Whether this viewpoint is empirically correct is actually irrelevant to the themes already addressed in earlier chapters. For I have emphasised the need to avoid the indulgence of inconsequential controversy as between one false dichotomy and another, e.g. Europe/the world, sovereignty/interference, democracy/bureaucracy, etc. The central process of developing a European dimension, as in any properly conducted educational enterprise, is the commitment to critical inquiry. The real enemy to the pursuit of truth in this matter is zealous adherence to didactic fundamentalism.

The core process of critical thinking

I suggest critical thinking is both the means and the outcome of developing a European dimension, as much among pupils as among parents, policy makers and practitioners. To paraphrase Wittgenstein; developing a European dimension will be a battle against the bewitchment of our intelligence by means of ideology.

The battle ground lies in the conceptual territory described in chapter three. The armoury is common to all forms of reasoning; hence the futility of viewing 'Europe' as a type of curriculum bolt-on executive extra. It is a concept enabling a variety of subject matters to be taught. But principally it is a value laden term about which we must reflect, judge and act critically (McPeck, 1981).

What does this imply? It implies that both reason and rationality must govern its provision. It presupposes that the unexamined life is not worth living and that as a consequence generalisations, plans and rules are necessary. Access to the examined life cannot proceed without scepticism of claims to authority least of all those based upon personal witness. These demands will necessarily require a denial of egocentricity and this in turn will act as the condition which enables a search for examples and instances that disconfirm assertions. Two main principles will govern this process; no distinctions without differences and respect for persons.

All of this need not be considered a passionless business. Feelings of care will be called for in bringing order into chaos and a concern for truth will motivate its pursuit. Learning to love one's enemy is akin to learning to live with the emotions engendered in encountering opposition to such forms of enquiry (Peters, 1973; Elliott, 1974). The core of the enterprise of developing a European dimension will involve a palpable tension. And it is perhaps a desire to reduce this tension or indeed a failure to recognise it as necessary that infects all denials of teaching for educational values.

The conflict arises from two essential elements; conformity to a process of reasoning in a given subject and operating with the facts, standards of judgement, and conventions that define it, and criticism of the validity of one or several of those elements. An attachment to conformity alone will end in bigotry; an over-reliance on criticism will issue in licence. As Hudson (1977) puts it 'criticism short of licence necessarily involves conformity to some standards. Conformity short of bigotry necessarily subjects standards to applications which might discredit them'.

So teachers and developers of a European dimension will have to accept that if they are to educate as distinct from school or indoctrinate, they will have to adopt a form of dialogue which will mean rejecting the safe havens of either/or thinking and embarking upon the high seas of both/and reasoning. For neither one nor the other can dominate in constructing this particular curriculum but always the one and the other. In short, the preferred method of teaching about Europe will require what Elliott (1975) has termed 'procedural neutrality'; a teacher's commitment not to use authority to promote judgements which cannot stand the test of reasoned appeal to validated evidence.[2]

The teacher–developer and networking

What chance has this philosophising about the role of the teacher–developer of the European dimension got of being put into practice? Attention has already been drawn to the problem of overload currently facing schools. Against this threat I have posed the opportunities presented through whole school development planning. But this approach, to transforming theory into practice will not work without continuing dialogue, the necessary condition for critical thinking. This 'active process of communication to the mutual enrichment of each' (Council of Europe, 1982) applies as much to teacher and taught as it must also do to our partners in any community of enquirers who have committed themselves to a tradition in which statements are to be challenged as to their adequacy.

So we must prioritise action, not in the initial stages towards content but towards process. The chief purpose must be to maximise dialogue with our partners in Europe from whatever region, country, nation or culture seems appropriate to the end of developing international understanding. The essential concept here in encouraging dialogue is networking.[3] By this I mean practitioners and the agencies which support them enabling structured and systematic dialogue to take place at a number of levels both within and between points of contact in the various European educational systems. It can be enhanced by various applications of technology (Bell and Dennis, 1991). But its key characteristic is an ethical commitment to create a community of interests where what is held in common is revised, evaluated and selectively acted upon.

Why networking? The justification for prioritising this action above all others is as follows:

- unity of purpose is secured and this is preferable to having differing intentions (solidarity),
- common interests encourage agreements in judgement (consensus),
- agreements are negotiated (contract),
- participants control the enterprise (autonomy),
- participants determine content (authority),
- outcomes are the corporate responsibility of the participants (accountability),

- the division of labour is related to the acknowledged competence of individuals (responsibility),
- outcomes are tested in action (confirmability),
- action is subject to reflection and deliberation (critical appraisal),
- action is evaluated in dialogue with participants (validation),
- actions which embody such processes, as outlined above, secure both education and training (emancipation).

On account of these factors, action networks especially when backed by research based teaching, necessarily represent an engagement in the development of mutual understanding. In short, schools must link with their counterparts in a framework of dialogue and critical thinking to ensure, minimally, the co-operation which the Single Market requires, and maximally to seize the opportunity of enhancing their own cultures through the enterprise of collaboration.[4]

Conclusion

I have attempted to address the challenge of developing a European dimension in the curriculum of primary schools. In doing so, I have offered some perspectives on the nature of educating for European citizenship. I have argued that both traditional pedagogy and prevailing assumptions about the nature of the teacher's role need to be re-examined. Reform through the ballot box is no safeguard against the tyranny of the majority. Our current experience of innovation in the U.K. should not delude us into believing that an attachment to a re-vitalised National Curriculum will not lead us either into subject chauvinism or worse, innovation without change.

If we are to realise the common ground, between those who seek to instruct for the needs of a common market place and those who embark upon the infinitely more difficult task of educating future Europeans, then certain preoccupations will be mandatory. The themes I have introduced, to meet these requirements, have been described in terms of:

Collaboration: linking levels within and between systems.
Participation: encouraging involvement among pupils, parents, teachers, trainers, advisers, inspectors, researchers, policy makers, etc.
Evaluation: generating evidence and data on the costs and benefits of a variety of programmes, resources usage, materials and approaches.
Dissemination: creating systematic opportunities to share and compare knowledge and experience.

In presenting this case I am conscious of a variety of propositions that require further justification. I have however proposed that seven teaching and learning processes to do with developing personal and national identity, citizenship, education for the global environment, economic and industrial understanding, inter-cultural and international education need to be brought into a structured relationship in order to create a critical mass to facilitate both action and research. For perpetuating current strategies will fail to meet the pre-conditions necessary for inter-cultural education to succeed. The proper corrective to extend the frontiers of existing educational practice in 1992 and beyond must be to forego the uses to which power-knowledge is put. We must moderate attempts, wherever they may appear in European education systems, to coerce and prematurely shape our future citizens through the arts of punishment, surveillance and unilateral examination. We must persist with and re-affirm our belief in the opposite path of knowledge-power in which the aim of enlightenment is attained through patiently supporting pupils to attain maturity through the use of reason. Such efforts must be backed by training, resources and an entitlement to a common curriculum in developing a European dimension to commence in the early years and extend through to secondary and higher education. In this way we will prepare pupils not only for citizenship but for the necessary virtues of courage and autonomy in performing the roles and duties of becoming a European in a newly democratised inter-cultural Europe.

Notes and References

Chapter 1

1. Comprehensive coverage of the detail of European educational policy making may be found in Neave (1984), Mickel (1986) and Galton and Blyth (1989).

2. The Council of Europe is the widest intergovernmental and inter-parliamentary grouping in Europe with 29 countries having signed the European Cultural Convention namely: Austria, Belgium, Cyprus, Czechoslovakia, Denmark, Germany, Finland, France, Greece, the Holy See, Hungary, Iceland, Ireland, Italy, Liechtenstein, Luxembourg, Malta, Netherlands, Norway, Poland, Portugal, San Marino, Spain, Sweden, Switzerland, Turkey, United Kingdom, Union of Soviet Socialist Republics and Yugoslavia.

3. D.E.S. Circulars 24/89, 59/89, contain a specific reference to the European dimension in relation to criteria which all teacher training institutions must meet in section 6.6.2 and section 6 para. 4 of the commentary.

4. Resolution of the Ministers of Education meeting within the Council, December 13th 1976, Official Journal, December 20th 1976 para. iv, section 5.

5. Presently there are at least four focal points of the Treaty of Rome for this issue to be contested. For example, Article 128 provides for the Council (acting by a simple majority only) to 'lay down general principles for implementing a common vocational training policy'. Virtually the whole of higher education has since been interpreted as being covered by the term vocational training. Article 48 establishes the right to free movement for workers within the Community and extends to the education of children of migrant workers. Article 57 provides for the mutual recognition of diplomas and certificates to facilitate the free movement of labour. The provision includes teachers who previously had to depend upon an idiosyncratic mix of

regulations and bureaucratic delay in gaining access to employment in E.C. schools. Article 7 prohibits any discrimination on grounds of nationality including access to vocational training to the extent that students from other E.C. countries currently have their fees paid by the U.K. government. Article 235 is an enabling clause, consistent with the base of the Treaty being specifically open to enlargement, which allows the Commission to propose action which is by agreement necessary to achieving its objectives for which the Treaty does not specifically provide powers.

Finally, there is the possibility of voluntary co-operation outside the scope of the Treaty. If all twelve Member States agree to a Resolution, then this will define initiatives that will then be jointly implemented.

A further aspect of E.C. involvement in education is the extension of existing initiatives to countries other than Member States, e.g. the TEMPUS programme which promotes mobility amongst students in higher education being made available to certain countries of Eastern Europe (cf: Saville, C. 'Britain in Europe: Community Co-operation in Education', British Council Seminar, 12th June 1990).

6. Action on this Resolution was outlined to operate at both Member State and Commission levels. It was agreed that:

within the limits of their own specific educational policies and structures the Member States will make every effort to implement the following measures:

Incorporation of the European dimension in educational systems:

- to set out in a document their current policies for incorporation of the European dimension in education and make this available to schools and other educational institutions;
- to encourage meaningful initiatives in all sectors of education aimed at strengthening the European dimension in education;

School programmes and teaching:

- to include the European dimension explicitly in their school curricula in all appropriate disciplines, for example literature, languages, history, geography, social sciences, economics and the arts.

Teaching material:

- to make arrangements so that teaching material takes account of the the common objective of promoting the European dimension.

Teacher training to give greater emphasis to the European dimension in teachers' initial and in-service training:

- making suitable teaching material available;
- access to documentation on the Community and its policies;
- provision of basic information on the educational systems of the other Member States;
- co-operation with teacher training institutions in other Member States, particularly by developing joint programmes providing for student and teacher mobility;
- making provision in the framework of in-service training for specific activities to enhance serving teachers' awareness of the European dimension in education and give them the opportunity of keeping up-to-date with Community developments;
- opening up, to some teachers from other Member States, certain in-service training activities which would constitute the practical expression of belonging to Europe and be a significant means of favouring the integration process.

Promotion of measures to boost contacts between pupils and teachers from different countries:

- to encourage contacts and meetings across borders between pupils and teachers from different Member States at all levels in order to give them direct experience of European integration and the realities of life in other European countries;
- to use these contacts and meetings both for improving linguistic proficiency and for gaining knowledge and experience on cultural, scientific and technical matters; in this way the largest possible number of young people and teachers should be covered by these initiatives;
- to encourage parents and parents' organisations to participate in organising contacts, exchanges and visits;
- to provide information and advice to schools, teachers and pupils interested in contacts, exchanges and visits abroad and to support them in the implementation of contacts and exchanges;
- to examine the conditions for longer-term stays abroad by pupils and to promote such stays abroad.

Complementary measures:

- to give a new stimulus in the perspective of 1992 to the strengthening of the image of Europe in education, in the sense of the People's Europe report, by organising particular events; in this connection the following would appear appropriate;
- colloquia and seminars on effective ways of introducing the European dimension in education and on the use and preparation of teaching material adapted to the different levels of teaching;
- the promotion of school initiatives and extra-curricular activities

such as school twinning and the formation of 'European clubs', opening up new paths for the strengthening of the European dimension;

- the participation of schools in activities organised as part of the Europe Day (May 9th);
- the participation of schools in the European schools' competition and encouragement of co-operation between competitions in the linguistic, artistic, scientific or technical fields organised in individual Member States;
- increased co-operation between the Member States in the area of school sports. (Commission of European Communities, 24th May 1988)

7. The programmes and policies of the Task Force were outlined in a Eurydice European Unit publication in 1989. A recent account of the work of the Task Force is described by its Director, Hywell Ceri Jones in the N.U.T. Education Review, Spring, 1990.

8. The case studies arising from the project have since been published by PAVIC publications, Sheffield City Polytechnic, Sheffield. There are nine currently available (see Chapter 2 below).

9. Whilst every effort has been taken to ensure accuracy, it should be noted that descriptions of policy and practice contained in this and subsequent chapters does not imply endorsement of the views expressed by the Commission of the European Communities or any other organisation, institution or agency identified.

Chapter 2

1. The contents of this chapter are drawn from: Bell and Lloyd (1989); Bell et al. (1989); Scurati (1989); Letiche (1990); Galesloot and Ten Brinke (1989); Kasper et al. (1990); Grass et al. (1990); Koval-Gillard (1990); Garcon and Prat (1990).

2. There is an extensive literature on issues surrounding practitioner research. Some recent publications include: Nias and Groundwater-Smith (1988); Carr and Kemmis (1986); Elliott (1991); Oja and Smulyan (1989); Winter (1989); Hitchcock and Hughes (1989); and Webb (1990).

3. The experience of the T.V.E.I. and Schools/Industry projects could usefully be drawn upon to examine ways in which these links could be further developed.

4. The Central Bureau for Educational Visits and Exchanges can provide a number of informative publications including 'Euro-Education News' and 'Edit: European Dimensions in Teaching'.

140

Chapter 3

1. The background to this issue can be traced through the various publications of the Politics Association and in particular the report of the Hansard Society's project (Crick and Porter, 1978) and a special issue of the Cambridge Journal of Education, on Political Education, Vol. 8, Nos. 2 and 3, 1978.

2. I am indebted to Christine Winter, advisory teacher for the European dimension, Sheffield L.E.A. for her interest and co-operation.

3. Ray Kirtley, Advisory Teacher for the European Dimension, Humberside L.E.A. provided invaluable help and assistance in compiling this account.

4. A fuller account is reported in EDIT, No. 1, Spring 1991. I particularly wish to acknowledge the support and assistance of Nigel Stewart, General Adviser, Doncaster L.E.A. who co-directed this project.

5. Gill Johnson provided an indispensible contribution in alerting teachers to the resources available. This support illustrates the benefits to be derived from close co-operation with the Libraries Service.

6. An outline of this project is provided in EDIT No. 1, Spring 1991.

Chapter 4

1. The School Development Plans project (D.E.S., 1989) provides some further elaboration of the themes explored in this chapter.

2. Guidelines for Review and Internal Development in Schools is a carefully structured school-based review process tested in a large number of primary and secondary schools in fifteen trial L.E.A.s. The process guides teachers on a whole school basis to examine the work of their school with a view to improvement. It is a thorough and systematic means of providing a situational analysis for development planning.

3. The general background to educational change is comprehensively described by Fullan (1982).

4. **N.G.T.** (Nominal Group Technique). This is a method of group evaluation for identifying issues and arriving at a consensus view whilst minimising conflict. The term 'nominal' indicates that the group need not have a permanent membership nor have a specific leader. The main advantage of the procedure is that it successfully equalises opportunities for individuals at whatever level in a hierarchy to express

their judgements. The technique is described in O'Neil (1981) and O'Neil and Jackson (1983).

D.I.O.N. (Diagnosing Individual and Organisational Needs). An approach for identifying staff development and training needs at the organisational rather than individual level. The basic tool is an inventory of sixty-six statements that individuals assess in relation to the school as a whole. It is very easy to use and is highly participative. The technique is described in Elliott-Kemp and Williams (1980).

Self evaluation. There are many check lists for carrying out a self assessment of performance. A comprehensive review of this technique was carried out in 1980 for the Schools Council by Elliott (1980).

School review. Several instruments have been developed along check list lines to evaluate whole school functioning. One of the most readable and useful was published by the I.L.E.A. (1982).

Chapter 5

1. Quoted in Jean Monnet *A Grand Design for Europe*, Commission of the European Community (1988).

2. The work of the Humanities Curriculum Project is an outstanding example of this approach (Stenhouse, 1983). See also Singh (1989) who argues that teachers must be committed to moral values in their teaching of certain social issues.

3. The relation of this concept to the wider issues of school based development is explored in Bell and Pennington (1988).

4. Increasing interest in teacher and pupil mobility is being encouraged through various exchange schemes. Electronic means of curriculum and school linking is also developing rapidly (see Beddis and Mares, 1988; Council of Europe, 1989; Austin, 1990).

Appendices

Appendix 1: E.C. resolutions, decisions and directives bearing on education

Council Decision of 2 April 1963 laying down general principles for implementing a common vocational training policy.

Resolution of the Ministers for Education meeting within the Council of 16 November 1971 on co-operation in the field of education.

Resolution of the Ministers for Education meeting within the Council of 6 June 1974 concerning co-operation in the field of education.

Council Resolution of 6 June 1974 on the mutual recognition of diplomas, certificates and other evidence of formal qualifications.

Resolution of the Council and of the Ministers for Education meeting within the Council of 9 February 1976 comprising an action programme in the field of education.

Resolution of the Council and of the Ministers for Education meeting within the Council of 13 December 1976 concerning measures to be taken to improve the preparation of young people for work and to facilitate their transition from education to working life.

Council Directive of 25 July 1977 on the education of migrant workers' children.

Resolution of the Council of 18 December 1979 on linked work and training for young persons.

Resolution of the Council and of the Ministers for Education meeting within the Council of 15 January 1980 concerning measures to be taken to improve the preparation of young people for work and to facilitate their transition from education to working life.

Resolution of the Council and of the Ministers for Education meeting within the Council of 12 July 1982 concerning measures to be taken to improve the preparation of young people for work and to facilitate their transition from education to working life.

Council Resolution of 2 June 1983 concerning vocational training measures relating to new information technologies.

Council Resolution of 11 July 1983 concerning vocational training policies in the European Community in the 1980s.

Resolution of the Council and of the Ministers for Education meeting within the Council of 19 September 1983 on measures relating to the introduction of new information technology in education.

Resolution of the Council and of the Ministers for Education meeting within the Council of 3 June 1985 containing the action programme on equal opportunities for girls and boys in education.

Resolution of the Council and the Ministers for Education meeting within the Council of 5 December 1985 extending for one year certain measures taken to improve the preparation of young people for work and to facilitate their transition from education to working life.

Resolution of the Council and of the Ministers for Education meeting within the Council of 9 June 1986 on consumer education in primary and secondary schools.

Council Decision of 24 July 1986 adopting the programme on co-operation between universities and enterprises regarding training in the field of technology (C.O.M.E.T.T.).

Council Decision of 15 June 1987 adopting the European Community action scheme for the mobility of university students (E.R.A.S.M.U.S.) (87/327/E.E.C.).

Council Decision of 1 December 1987 concerning an action programme for the vocational training of young people and their preparation for adult and working life (P.E.T.R.A.).

Council Decision of 18 April 1988 establishing a second Community action programme for disabled people (H.E.L.I.O.S.).

Resolution of the Council and the Ministers of Education meeting within the Council of 24 May 1988 on the European dimension in education.

Resolution of the Council and the Ministers for Education meeting within the Council of 24 May 1988 on environmental education.

Council Decision of 16 June 1988 adopting an action programme for the promotion of youth exchanges in the Community – 'Youth for Europe' programme.

Council Decision of 29 June 1988 on a Community action in the field of learning technologies – development of European learning through technological advance (D.E.L.T.A.).

144

Resolution of the Council and the Ministers for Education meeting within the Council of 23 November 1988 concerning health education in schools.

Council Decision of 16 December 1988 adopting the second phase of the programme on co-operation between universities and industry regarding training in the field of technology (C.O.M.E.T.T. II) (1990–4).

Council Directive of 21 December 1988, on a general system for the recognition of higher-education diplomas awarded on completion of professional education and training of at least three years' duration.

Resolution of the Council and Ministers of Education meeting within the Council of 22 May 1989 on school provision for gypsy and traveller children.

Resolution of the Council and Ministers for Education meeting within the Council of 22 May 1989 on school provision for children of occupational travellers.

Council Decision of 28 July 1989 establishing an action programme to promote foreign language competence in the E.C. (L.I.N.G.U.A.).

Council Decision of 14 December 1989 amending Decision 87/327/E.E.C. adopting the E.C. action scheme for the mobility of university students (E.R.A.S.M.U.S.).

Resolution of the Council and Ministers for Education meeting within the Council of 14 December 1989 on measures to combat failure at school.

Resolution of the Council and Ministers of Education meeting within the Council of 31 May 1990 on integration of children and young people with disabilities into ordinary systems of education.

Source: Central Bureau for Educational Visits and Exchanges (1990) European Awareness Pilot Project. London. Central Bureau.

Appendix 2: Possible and desirable measures towards developing a European dimension: an edited selection of suggestions

1. Giving a European dimension to teachers and pupils' experience

● Exchanges, recognition of periods of study, European/international institutions established
● Short study visits
● Initial teacher training undertaken for part of duration in another Member State
● Intensive contacts with other training institutions developed
● Bi-lateral and multi-lateral programmes of study introduced
● International meetings of teachers
● Improved access to data-bases of resources and training materials
● Establishing book and materials repositories
● Encouraging and liaising with voluntary agencies.

2. At Member State level

● Identifying European dimension in school curricula and teacher training
● Provision of in-service training opportunities
● Funded exchange programmes
● Initiate teaching materials development
● Establish co-ordination group.

3. At Commission level

● Encourage school/pupil contacts and exchanges
● Evaluate implementation of current policies and redefine objectives
● Review progress in initial teacher training courses
● Examine access to documentation on the Community for teachers
● Consider content of common course on the Community process and related texts
● Disseminate examples of good practice
● Encourage links between educational research establishments
● Develop handbooks for facilitating school contacts and exchanges.

Source: Commission Report (1987) Greater Emphasis for the European Dimension in Education.

Appendix 3: European awareness: key stages one to three

(*N.B.* The attainment targets quoted below were based on the *Interim Reports*)

European awareness in key stage one

Schools should consider ways of teaching pupils to:

ASPECTS OF THE EUROPEAN DIMENSION	CURRICULUM CONTEXTS IN WHICH THESE ASPECTS MIGHT BE DEVELOPED	LINKS TO N.C. SUBJECTS
Acquire an understanding of European geography	After background experience with a world map and/or satellite photographs pupils are encouraged to focus on the map of Europe. They begin to identify countries, seas and mountain ranges from an atlas or wallmap.	Geog. A.T. 1 Science A.T. 12
Develop an understanding of language and culture in a European context	Pupils listen and respond to folk tales and stories. Many of these are trans-European and represent a shared heritage.	Eng. A.T. 1
Take part in and appreciate the benefits of links of all kinds with other European countries	Pupils encounter a visitor to school who has a European language other than English as their mother tongue. They follow this meeting by collecting stamps, coins and other artifacts from the country concerned.	Eng. A.T. 1 Geog. A.T. 1 and 2 Maths A.T. 8

ASPECTS OF THE EUROPEAN DIMENSION	CURRICULUM CONTEXTS IN WHICH THESE ASPECTS MIGHT BE DEVELOPED	LINKS TO N.C. SUBJECTS
Understand the growing economic interdepend-ence between European countries	A study of diet and health provides an opportunity to look at other European countries as sources of foodstuffs for a varied and interesting diet.	Science A.T. 3 Geog. A.T. 4
Recognise the links which exist between Europe and the rest of the world	Pupils identify some of the raw materials and resources on which Europe depends but which come from outside the continent e.g. tropical hardwoods.	Science A.T. 6 Tech. A.T. 2 and 3 Geog. A.T. 4
Develop an understanding of European history including the evolution of the E.C.	Pupils discuss groups and the activities carried on in them. This leads to the idea of the E.C. as a co-operative organisation and to the stages in its development.	Maths A.T. 3 Eng. A.T. 1 Geog. A.T. 1 and 2 Hist. A.T. 1
Appreciate the indivisible nature of European environmental issues and problems	A study of a conservation project in the school grounds or local area could lead to an opportunity to consider conservation in Europe either as a general concept or focused on another local project (perhaps around a twinned school).	Science A.T. 5 Geog. A.T. 5

ASPECTS OF THE EUROPEAN DIMENSION	CURRICULUM CONTEXTS IN WHICH THESE ASPECTS MIGHT BE DEVELOPED	LINKS TO N.C. SUBJECTS
Develop an increased awareness of the daily lives of other Europeans	Using books, photographs or video for background information pupils create material which illustrates a day in the life of a contemporary from another European country.	Geog. A.T. 4 Eng. A.T. 1–3 Art R.E. Drama

Source: Draft Consultation Document: Humberside L.E.A. (1990)

European awareness in key stage two

ASPECTS OF THE EUROPEAN DIMENSION	CURRICULUM CONTEXTS IN WHICH THESE ASPECTS MIGHT BE DEVELOPED	LINKS TO N.C. SUBJECTS
Acquire an understanding of European geography	Pupils begin to make their own maps of Europe showing countries, capital cities and important physical features. This leads to work with compass and scale.	Geog. A.T. 1 Science A.T. 9
Develop an understanding of language and culture in a European context	Pupils conduct a survey of European languages spoken within the school/class/ family. They investigate the relationships and similarities between different European languages through the medium of a simple foreign shopping expedition.	Eng. A.T. 1–3 Maths A.T. 3 and 8

ASPECTS OF THE EUROPEAN DIMENSION	CURRICULUM CONTEXTS IN WHICH THESE ASPECTS MIGHT BE DEVELOPED	LINKS TO N.C. SUBJECTS
Take part in and appreciate the benefits of links of all kinds with other European countries	Pupils discuss forming a class link with a similar group in another European country. The class selects and constructs material to send to their linked group. They investigate the means by which information is transmitted throughout Europe.	Eng. A.T. 1 Science A.T. 12
Understanding the growing economic interdependence between European countries	Pupils survey the countries of origin of vehicles or electrical appliances. They graph their results and plot the locations of factories and likely trade routes on maps of Europe.	Geog. A.T. 4 Maths A.T. 12
Recognise the links which exist between Europe and the rest of the world	Using tables, lists or databases pupils extract specific pieces of information. E.g. flights from European capitals to destinations outside of Europe.	Maths A.T. 12 Geog. A.T. 1
Develop an understanding of European history including the evolution of the E.C.	Pupils investigate the various waves of invasion and migration which have helped to shape present day Europe in terms of language, culture and customs.	Hist. A.T. 1–4 Geog. A.T. 1

ASPECTS OF THE EUROPEAN DIMENSION	CURRICULUM CONTEXTS IN WHICH THESE ASPECTS MIGHT BE DEVELOPED	LINKS TO N.C. SUBJECTS
Appreciate the indivisible nature of European environmental issues and problems	Pupils conduct a survey of the variety and distribution of fauna and flora found within Europe. This leads to an investigation of threatened European habitats.	Science A.T. 2 Geog. A.T. 1 Maths A.T. 12
Develop an increased awareness of the daily lives of other Europeans	Pupils focus their attention on groups of Europeans living outside of their country of origin (perhaps within the local area). They identify their reasons for moving and the distances involved. They consider the problems of being a member of a minority group and think about their own attitudes to minorities.	Eng. A.T. 1–3 Geog. A.T. 4 Maths A.T. 12 R.E.

Source: Draft Consultation Document: Humberside L.E.A. (1990)

European awareness in key stage three

ASPECTS OF THE EUROPEAN DIMENSION	CURRICULUM CONTEXTS IN WHICH THESE ASPECTS MIGHT BE DEVELOPED	LINKS TO N.C. SUBJECTS
Acquire an understanding of ⌐uropean geography	Using data in the form of a database or tables pupils investigate climatic variation across Europe and relate this to aspects of human geography e.g. agriculture.	Science A.T. 9 Geog. A.T. 1–4 Maths A.T. 12

ASPECTS OF THE EUROPEAN DIMENSION	CURRICULUM CONTEXTS IN WHICH THESE ASPECTS MIGHT BE DEVELOPED	LINKS TO N.C. SUBJECTS
Develop an understanding of language and culture in a European context	Pupils collect material with the aim of planning and constructing a language and cultural taster pack for use by younger members of their school or feeder primary. This might include basic phrases, recorded music, media items or material from tourist offices. Tech POS: Work with a variety of media to produce (e.g.) an information pack.	Eng. A.T. 1–3 Tech. A.T. 1–3 Lang. A.T. 1 and 3
Take part in and appreciate the benefits of links of all kinds with other European countries	Pupils plan and develop a project in association with a linked school in Europe. A local discovery trail might be an example. Where appropriate electronic mail could be used between schools.	Lang. A.T. 3 and 4 Eng. A.T. 3 Hist. A.T. 1 and 3 Geog. A.T. 1 and 2
Understand the growing economic interdependence between European countries	A study of the tourist industry in Europe. Pupils conduct surveys of class/school holiday destinations in Europe, consider the attractions of various destinations and the impact of mass tourism. They share their findings.	Geog. A.T. 1 and 3 Science A.T. 9 Maths A.T. 12

152

ASPECTS OF THE EUROPEAN DIMENSION	CURRICULUM CONTEXTS IN WHICH THESE ASPECTS MIGHT BE DEVELOPED	LINKS TO N.C. SUBJECTS
Recognise the links which exist between Europe and the rest of the world	Pupils are asked to collect news items or magazine articles which focus on the relationship between Europe and less Developed Countries. They investigate the implications of these relationships in terms of (e.g.) food aid, arms sales or dumping of toxic waste.	Eng. A.T. 1–3 Science A.T. 5 Geog. A.T. 4 and 5
Develop an understanding of European history including the evolution of the E.C.	Geog. POS: Pupils should consider the reasons for and the aims of the E.C.	Geog. A.T. 4 Hist. A.T. 3
Appreciate the indivisible nature of European environmental issues and problems	Geog. POS: Pupils should investigate an environmental issue in a European region and be able to explain the effects of E.C. policies.	Geog. A.T. 5 Science A.T. 5
Develop an increased awareness of the daily lives of other Europeans	Geog. POS: Pupils should examine spacial variation in economic prosperity and the quality of life in a selected E.C. country by a comparative study of two of its regions.	Geog. A.T. 4

Source: Draft Consultation Document: Humberside L.E.A. (1990)

Appendix 4: Mapping the European dimension at key stages one and two in the National Curriculum core subjects: English, mathematics and science (based on the *Interim Reports*)

English key stage one

A.T. 1 – SPEAKING AND LISTENING

Levels 1 and 2	Opportunity to listen, and respond to stories from a variety of cultural sources. (Many of our basic folk tales are 'European' – shared heritage e.g. Goldilocks, Cinderella).
Levels 1 and 2	Role play e.g. customer/waiter – fish and chip shop, bistro, pizza parlour, etc.
Levels 2 and 3	Participate in a group in a given task, e.g. design related activity such as windmills (Spain, Greece, Holland) linking with Science A.T. 10 (Forces) and A.T. 13 (Energy). Any early study skills activity, e.g. sorting and classifying coins; using reference materials to identify European countries; flags, etc.
Levels 2 and 3	Describe an event – talk, listen, ask and answer questions, e.g. reporting back to class *any* group activity as above; discussing a T.V. programme or book (an increasing number of T.V. Schools' broadcasts reflect a variety of cultural backgrounds including Europe).

A.T. 2 – READING

Levels 1, 2 and 3	Using stories from a variety of cultural sources.
Level 2	Reading signs, labels and notices e.g. simple menus (parallel activity to role play A.T. 1).
Level 3	Using information sources and reference books, e.g. information about European countries, flags, etc.

A.T. 3 – WRITING

Levels 1, 2 and 3	Depict stories in pictorial and written form, e.g. link with A.T. 1 and A.T. 2 re. stories and folk tales from Europe.
Levels 2 and 3	Offer a chronological account of a known story, T.V. programme, etc., e.g. stories and folk tales of Europe.
Levels 2 and 3	Non-chronological writing, e.g. menus, posters, cards (link with role play – A.T. 1).

A.T. 1 – SPELLING AND A.T. 5 – HANDWRITING

Opportunities would arise in relation to the topic or theme. Ideally this would parallel A.T.s 1, 2, and 3.

Mathematics key stages one and two

A.T. 1 – USING AND APPLYING MATHEMATICS

Level 1
: Make predictions based on experience, e.g. comparison of weights of two objects such as fruits or veg. e.g. aubergine (European foods).

Levels 2 to 5
: Select the materials and the mathematics to use for a task e.g.

1. use string to measure the circumference of e.g. an Edam cheese;
2. design a board game based on the map of Europe that uses coordinates.

A.T.s 2 and 3 – NUMBER

Levels 1 to 5
: Understand number and number notation and operations.
  This gives an opportunity to portray number notation as an internationally understood language.

A.T. 4 – NUMBER

Levels 1 to 5
: Estimate and approximate in number.
  Estimations of tasks such as those in A.T. 1.

A.T. 7 - ALGEBRA

Levels 4 and 5	Use coordinates to plot points and draw diagrams. This links with the use of maps, e.g. the board game, A.T. 1.

A.T. 8 - MEASURES

Level 1	Mathematical language, e.g. wider, heavy, hot – link with A.T. 1 and science A.T. 1.
Level 2	Using coins in simple context. This offers the opportunity to see similarities in European decimal currency systems.
Level 4	Use timetables to anticipate time of arrival, e.g. cross-channel ferries; planes to European destinations.
Level 5	Understand notation of scale in maps – offers the opportunity to use scale to work out distances in Europe, e.g. a car journey from one city to another; an air route.

A.T. 9 - USING AND APPLYING MATHS

Level 2	Sorting and classifying, e.g. a set of European coins or stamps.
Levels 4 and 5	Record findings and present them in oral, written or visual form, e.g.

1. block graph of preferences re. a variety of European recipes;
2. investigation of country of origin of family cars – presentation as chart, graph or diagram (link with map). Test a statement such as more of our cars were made in Europe than outside of Europe.

A.T. 10 - SHAPE AND SPACE

Two dimensional and three dimensional shape. Offers the opportunity to explore the flat map in relation to the glob.

A.T. 11 – SHAPE AND SPACE

Level 4	Location by means of coordinates, e.g. capital cities of Europe.
Level 5	Use networks to solve problems, e.g. find the shortest road route between two given European cities.

A.T. 12 – HANDLING DATA

Level 1	Select criteria for sorting a set of objects, e.g. European coins, stamps, categories of food.
Level 2	As above plus record results.
Levels 3 and 4	Extract specific pieces of information from tables and lists, e.g. flights from Manchester airport to destinations in Europe. Enter and access information in a simple database e.g. flight information; nouns across several European languages.

A.T. 13 – HANDLING DATA

Level 2	Construct, read and interpret block graphs e.g. coins, stamps, favourite recipes.
Level 3	As above – using bar charts.
Level 4	Create a decision-tree diagram to sort and identify, e.g. a set of coins, stamps, flags.

Science key stages one and two

A.T.1 – EXPLORATION OF SCIENCE

Levels 1 to 5	Observing, describing and recording, e.g. 1. changes in foodstuffs during cooking – for instance pasta; 2. varieties of breads from basic dough – pizza, french stick, croissant, pitta.

A.T. 1 – THE VARIETY OF LIFE

Level 5 — Physical factors between localities reflect in the different species – opportunity for comparative study of flora and fauna of Europe.

A.T. 3 – PROCESSES OF LIFE

Levels 1 to 4 — A study based on flowers/plants could centre on bulbs from Holland and include detailed observation drawing, microscope study of parts of flower, paintings, etc.

Levels 2 to 5 — A study of diet and health offers the opportunity to look at our interdependence with other European countries for a varied and interesting diet. Food origins and sources outside the U.K.

A.T. 4 – GENETICS AND EVOLUTION

Levels 1 to 5 — Illustrate variety of life as the natural state. Useful concept to cross-relate with variety of culture.

A.T. 5 – HUMAN INFLUENCES ON THE EARTH

Levels 3 and 5 — Offer the opportunity to link with the need for legislation re. pollution control and environmental issues and the E.C. regulations that affect our lives in these areas.

A.T. 6 – TYPES AND USES OF MATERIALS

Levels 1 to 4 — A study of the properties of materials could be based on or include traditional uses or cultural artefacts, e.g. a study of clogs — from Lancashire cotton mills, Yorkshire fells, steelworks, Holland – could reflect on the comparative properties of wood, steel, leather and their suitability in each context.

A.T. 9 – EARTH AND ATMOSPHERE

Level 3   Using common meteorological symbols as used in the media. This offers the opportunity of using maps as a background e.g. satellite pictures of Europe.

Level 3   Effect of weathering on the landscape. An opportunity for introducing this occurs from a study of the effect of climate and is illustrated superbly by colour prints of Europe viewed from satellite.

A.T. 10 – FORCES

Level 4   Investigation of wind-powered models, e.g. windmills (Greece, Spain, Holland).

A.T. 11 – ELECTRICITY AND MAGNETISM

Levels 1 to 5   Opportunity to note country of origin of electrical goods in the home.

A.T. 12 – SCIENTIFIC ASPECTS OF INFORMATION

Levels 1 to 4   Study of information via satellite, e.g. map of Europe, weather patterns.

A.T. 13 – ENERGY

Level 1   Food as an energy source – links with A.T. 1 and A.T. 3. Opportunity for cross-curricular study of food including country of origin (see English key stage one).

Levels 2 to 4   Energy sources – strengthening of opportunities in A.T. 10 and English A.T. 1.

A.T. 14 – SOUND AND MUSIC

Levels 1 to 3   Sounds produced in a variety of ways by a variety of instruments. This offers the opportunity to introduce the instruments, sounds and music of other cultures, e.g. Bazooki, Flamenco, British Folk instruments.

A.T. 16 – THE EARTH IN SPACE

Level 2   Knowledge of the solar system; the earth as a
                 planet.

Levels 4 and 5   Offers the opportunity and the background
                 knowledge to study land shapes (continents) and
                 introduce geographical information of Europe.

Appendix 5: Topic web of curricular activities

TALKING

DISCUSSIONS – REASONS FOR LEARNING FRENCH
A COMMON EUROPEAN LANGUAGE
A COMMON CURRENCY
(CONVERSIONS)

DEBATES – POCKET MONEY (BUDGET)
– CORPORAL PUNISHMENT (E.C. RULE)
– ENVIRONMENTAL ISSUE (CHOICE)

INTERVIEWING SKILLS –M.P./M.E.P. VISITOR
OTHER PUPILS/VISITORS

FRENCH – COMMUNICATION SKILLS DEVELOPED

LISTENING

LOCAL M.P./M.E.P. INVITED TO TALK
CHILDREN INVITED TO SHARE EXPERIENCE
OF OTHER EDUCATIONAL SYSTEMS

MEMBERS COMMUNITY/INDUSTRY
INVITED TO SHARE EXPERTISE
RESPONSE TO INSTRUCTIONS IN FRENCH

LANGUAGE ARTS

WRITING

MYSELF AND OTHER PEOPLE – REASONS FOR
WRITING

TOPIC SPELLING

WORD DERIVATIONS – (LATIN/FRENCH) ROOTS

ABBREVIATIONS G.A.T.T., L.O.M.E., E.R.D.F.,
E.C.U., E.C.S.C. etc.

READING

REFERENCE AND HIGHER READING SKILLS

CONSTANTLY BEING DEVELOPED
THROUGHOUT TOPIC
CURRENT PAMPHLETS AND INFORMATION
SELECTED HOLIDAY BROCHURES
SELECTED PAGES 'EUROPE – MAPS AND
MAPWORK'

MOUNTAIN RESCUE – PAST TENSE; WORD PROCESSED STORY

RESCUER AND INJURED PARTY = DIALOGUE (DIRECT SPEECH)

INSTRUCTIONS – HOW TO MAKE PIZZA

COMPLILING QUESTIONS – INTERVIEWS

ORGANISING ARGUMENTS – DEBATES

NOTE TAKING – DEBATES

LETTER-WRITING – TO OTHER COUNTRIES TO FORGE LINKS AND GATHER INFORMATION

READING FOR INFORMATION

– ORGANISING A SKI TRIP
– ABBREVIATIONS
– DICTIONARIES

COMPARING DIFFERENT FORMS OF LANGUAGE –

ADVERTS, DICTIONARIES, FICTION NEWS

RECREATIONAL READING INCLUDES OTHER CHILDREN'S REVIEWS

HISTORY

E.C.
REASONS FOR ESTABLISHMENT
WINSTON CHURCHILL
ROBERT SCHUMAN
JEAN MONNET
MEMBERSHIP GROWTH
INSULARITY OF BRITAIN

GEOGRAPHY

MEMBER – PEOPLE/LANGUAGE
STATES   SHAPE/LOCATION
            CAPITAL/FLAG
            CURRENCY/STAMPS
            INDUSTRIES/POP
+ SELECTED PAGES 'EUROPE
    MAPS AND MAPWORK'

SOCIAL EDUCATION

POLITICAL STRUCTURE
ELECTORAL PROCEDURES
ATTITUDES
STEREO-TYPING?
DOMINANT RELIGIONS
COMPARISON OF
   CUSTOMS/BELIEFS
EDUCATION

ENVIRONMENTAL STUDIES

MATHS

E.C. *BUDGET* TO BE PRODUCED

FOREIGN CURRENCY BILLS
          CONVERSION
          E.C.U.

GRAPHS – FORMS OF ENERGY IN THE HOME
ROUTES – TRAVELLING TIME AND DISTANCE

VALUE – ORGANISING A SKI TRIP

ORIENTEERING – *USING A COMPASS* – IN
MOUNTAIN RESCUE

DECIMALS – READING METERS

WEIGHING/MEASURING/COSTING PIZZA

SCIENCE

SOLAR ENERGY – CLASSROOM EXPERIMENTS
DEVISED BY CHILDREN USING
NORTH AND SOUTH-FACING
WINDOWS

POLLUTION   – IDENTIFYING AND REPORTING
            ON CARBON DIOXIDE
            EMISSIONS

HEALTH   – SMOKING – OBSERVATION AND
            REPORTING SKILLS

SAFETY   – PROTECTIVE CLOTHING

INVESTIGATING PROPERTIES OF DIFFERENT
MATERIALS

CREATING/BAKING PIZZA

GROUP PAPIER MÂCHÉ MODEL OF PARTICULAR
COUNTRY STUDIED

MAKING/COLOURING FLAGS

COIN RUBBINGS

POSTERS (1) ELECTORAL   (2) ENVIRONMENTAL

GET WELL CARD – 'MOUNTAIN RESCUE'

A 'COMMON LANGUAGE' STORY USING
PICTURES

COLLECTION DISPLAY OF FOODS/GOODS FROM
OTHER COUNTRIES

MUSIC

POP STARS/MUSIC IN OTHER COUNTRIES

FRENCH SONGS

AS OUTLINED
AND RESPONDING TO NUMBERS AND COLOURS
IN FRENCH

CREATIVE DANCE – USING SCOTTISH,
SPANISH AND GREEK MUSIC

EXPRESSIVE ARTS

DRAMA

ROLE PLAY – GOING THROUGH CUSTOMS

MEETING YOUR PEN-PAL
STRUCTURED SITUATION

TRY TO FIND A DOCTOR BECAUSE OF? –
MIME (ACCIDENT)

DIALOGUE BETWEEN RESCUER AND RESCUED
IN HOSPITAL AFTER ACCIDENT ON MOUNTAIN

FREE EXPRESSION

AVALANCHE!

Appendix 6: The topic of 'communication' and National Curriculum links

Autumn term 1989

KEY IDEAS	SKILLS	ACTIVITY/EXPERIENCE	A.T.
Know that U.K. and Europe are distinct regions on world map.	Observation Information Recording	Use of globe, atlas, satellite photographs in game activity to develop familiarity. Be able to locate U.K. and Europe on large map.	G.A.T. 2 G.A.T. 3
Land masses are divided into continent, country, island	Information Recording Social Classification	Identify on map, countries and major cities. Group activity. Learn to identify shapes and relative position. Discussion bases.	G.A.T. 5 E.A.T. 1
Doncaster is linked to other U.K. cities by rail network. Now electrified.	Investigative Problem solving Observation Recording	Mapwork showing routes. Route finding game. Distance work for more able. Electricity, safety.	G.A.T. 8 S.A.T. 11
People travel from Doncaster to many different places.	Investigative Questioning Classification Recording	Devise and administer questionnaire. Graph and map results. Computer to handle data. Use of tape-recorder.	E.A.T. 1 M.A.T. 12 M.A.T. 13 S.A.T. 12
Facilities exist to assist safe and comfortable travel.	Observation Classification	People at work; language and drama.	E.A.T. 1 E.A.T. 3
People are employed to ensure smooth running of railway.	Recording Investigative Social Communication	Discuss ways to improve facilities. Any problems for Euro-visitors? Design own signs for facilities.	G.A.T. 6 D.T.A.T.
Doncaster can be used to begin a rail-journey to Europe. It will soon be a Euro-Centre.	Information Problem solving Investigative Recording Manipulative	Use timetables, holiday brochures to discover European routes. Discuss idea of Channel link Devise own race game through Europe. Build feature for game	M.A.T. 12 S.A.T. 5 E.A.T. 1 D.T.A.T.

KEY IDEAS	SKILLS	ACTIVITY/EXPERIENCE	A.T.
Some European countries can be reached directly by rail/sea.	Observation Investigation Information	Investigate famous landmarks, features, buildings of some European countries.	G.A.T. 3 E.A.T. 2
European countries have different language and culture from ours.	Social Moral Aesthetic Communication Investigative Information	Opportunity for children's own investigations – language, currency, food, customs.	E.A.T. 1 E.A.T. 2 E.A.T. 3
Many European things are around us.	Observation Investigation Classification	Look for European influences locally. Cars, food, visitors. Mapwork. Trade routes.	G.A.T. 1 M.A.T. 12

Spring term 1990

KEY IDEAS	SKILLS	ACTIVITY/ EXPERIENCE	A.T.
Know that U.K. and Europe are distinct regions on world map.	Observation Information Recording	Use of globe, atlas, satellite photographs in game activity. Be able to locate U.K. and Europe	G.A.T. 2 G.A.T. 3
Land masses are divided into continents, countries and islands	Information Classification Recording Social skills	Identify on map, countries, cities, islands of Europe. Group activity to learn relative locations N.S.E.W.	G.A.T. 5 E.A.T. 1 M.A.T. 8
Doncaster is linked to other U.K. cities by a rail network – now electrified.	Investigative Problem solving Observation Recording	Mapwork of rail routes, route finding game, safety on the railway.	G.A.T. 8 S.C.A.T. 11
People travel from Doncaster to many different places.	Investigative Classification Problem solving Communication	Devise and administer questionnaire for people at railway station, graph and map results. Computer to handle data.	E.A.T. 1 M.A.T. 12 M.A.T. 13

KEY IDEAS	SKILLS	ACTIVITY/EXPERIENCE	A.T.
Facilities exist at the station for benefit of travellers.	Observation Classification Social Aesthetic	Chart showing signs of facilities – are they 'Euro-friendly' – role play.	E.A.T. 1 E.A.T. 3
People are employed to ensure smooth running of the railway.	Recording Observation Communication Investigative	Discuss importance of jobs at station. Design own signs for facilities.	G.A.T. 6 D.T.A.T. 1
A journey to Europe can begin from Doncaster station.	Information Recording Investigative Problem solving Manipulative	Use timetables, holiday brochures to discover Euro routes. Channel link. Devise own game through Europe.	M.A.T. 12 S.C.A.T. 5 E.A.T. 1 D.T.A.T. 2/3
Some European countries have direct rail and sea links with U.K.	Observation Investigation Recording	Use of appropriate maps, plotting routes, identifying destinations on large wall map.	G.A.T. 3
European countries have different languages and cultures.	Social Moral Communication Investigative	Children's own investigations from material received from embassies – language, currency, food, customs.	E.A.T. 1 E.A.T. 2 E.A.T. 3 E.A.T. 4
Many European things are around us in our daily lives.	Observation Investigation Social Moral Classification	Investigations in locality and the home. e.g. Cars – country of origin Food – labelling Wine – country of origin Mapping results.	G.A.T. 1 M.A.T. 8 M.A.T. 12 M.A.T. 13
Europe is a popular destination for holiday-makers from the U.K.	Information Investigation Classification Recording Observation Social Moral	Visit travel agent. Plan a holiday – cost, travel arrangements, likely weather, things to see. Currency, language. Each group give presentation to rest of class.	E.A.T. 1–5 G.A.T. 1 G.A.T. 3 M.A.T. 1 M.A.T. 3 M.A.T. 8 M.A.T. 9

N.B. The Attainment Targets cited above will require modification in the light of current developments.

Appendix 7: Communications topic: planning and developing a European dimension

Joint Schools Day Conference

↓

Pre-planning headteacher, deputy head, support teacher

↓

Year Group Planning

↓

Visits arranged. Contacts made

↓

Work began

Class 4   Class 5   Class 6

Input across all three classes from Teaching Support Service

↓

INTRODUCTORY ACTIVITIES

| Communicating locally – routeways around the village. | Different forms of communicating, e.g. sound. | Looking at the earth from space; land, sea, continents, boundaries. |

↓

VISIT TO DONCASTER RAILWAY STATION

| Questionnaire and data handling; destinations and reasons for travelling. | | Railway as a link to Europe. Suitability for Euro-visitors (signs). |

↓

| Use of globes and atlases to locate Britain and Europe. | Visit to engineering firm making Channel Tunnel trains. | Europe around us and in the home. |

Compare and contrast children's experiences.	European accessibility of major routes.	Local visits. Holiday destinations.

European information books; study skills.	Drama involving tunnel travel.	Local motor dealer – Alfa Romeo.

Goods from Europe. E. European countries.	Design problem; egg race from Kirn; West Germany.	Supermarket – food from Europe.

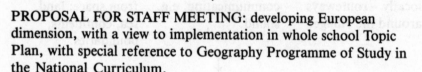

EXPERIENCES SHARED WITH THE WHOLE SCHOOL THROUGH CLASS ASSEMBLIES

↓

EVALUATION BY ALL STAFF INVOLVED IN PROJECT

↓

CASCADED TO WHOLE SCHOOL THROUGH PROJECT REPORT

↓

PROPOSAL FOR STAFF MEETING: developing European dimension, with a view to implementation in whole school Topic Plan, with special reference to Geography Programme of Study in the National Curriculum.

Appendix 8: 121 ideas for Europe in the classroom

1. Games devised from using small globes (with raised contours to indicate main features).
2. Games devised for outdoor or indoor use of giant inflatable globes (available from Hestair Hope).
3. Make dominoes, using flags and nationality car plates.
4. Using slides, posters and videos of the earth from space devise activities based on the theme of 'Europe in a Global Perspective' (obtain catalogue from National Remote Sensing Centre, Farnborough).
5. Devise simple Euroquiz based on famous persons, common expressions, major cities, geographical features, historical events, artistic masterpieces, architectural monuments, food, traditions, etc.
6. Vary the theme of Euroquiz by presenting the question in the form of crossword clues.
7. Produce a variety of maps: wall maps, wall pictures, drawing in school playground, carpet map, etc.
8. Build up different types of photographic collages: cities, monuments, flora, fauna, people, art objects, traditions, costumes, currency, etc.
9. Design and make 2D and 3D Eurosymbols based on some existing examples.
10. Devise activities which destroy existing stereotypes by providing some stock examples in a variety of media.
11. Devise word games from the names of some or all the countries of Europe.
12. Devise word games from the names of regions in single countries.
13. Organise pupils to interview each other about their contacts with other countries, the origins of their friends or relatives, and plot this on a 'personal history' map.
14. Encourage pupils to interview their relatives, especially parents and grandparents on their experience of other countries. Devise a route of their travels.
15. Encourage role play based on the experience of being different, isolated and in a minority situation.
16. Combat prejudice by selecting stories that portray the experience of being a stranger in a foreign land.
17. Collect pictures which show contrasting environments in Europe. Devise a series of prompts which highlight the chief environmental/historical/geographical/artistic concepts.
18. Identify capital cities of Europe from photographs of Europe taken from space.
19. Collect photos of famous buildings. Cut in half, thirds or quarters and devise a game of seeking the missing parts.

20. Make a collage of famous monuments and devise a quiz to pick out the main features.

21. Provide a scale map and supply instructions to calculate distances from specific points e.g. capital cities.

22. Make a hexagonal jigsaw with towns and countries.

23. Devise an outline map of the main motorways in Europe. Pose questions about specific routes. Set problems based upon travelling from one country, town or city to another. Calculate times and distances, costs, etc.

24. Make a collection of pictures showing different landscapes. Devise sorting activities based on geographical or geological concepts.

25. Take up annual European themes as these arise: conservation, tourism, environment, etc.

26. Collect packets and labels from European goods and stick them on a large map of Europe.

27. Ditto – using currencies.

28. Ditto – using stamps.

29. Make a large map of Europe with the help of an overhead projector.

30. Make a list of the countries of Europe. Ask pupils to identify the names of the main units of currency for each one.

31. Identify where the main European makes of motor car are manufactured and assembled on a map of Europe.

32. Collect pictures of European cars and pin them to a map showing their place or country of origin.

33. Devise a picture which conveys messages of the relation of Europe and the Third World. Invite pupils to devise a story of what they perceive.

34. Devise a European menu selecting dishes from each of the countries.

35. Devise a regional European menu by selecting dishes from the main regions of Europe.

36. Collect recipes and make one or more dishes.

37. Identify where there are foreign restaurants in the locality. Encourage pupils to talk to the owners, write down the menu, prepare a brochure on eating places and plot their origins.

38. Prepare a European menu for classmates with the help of parents from the country of origin.

39. Visit the local greengrocer or supermarket. Identify where different products and food come from.

40. Devise activities to develop economic and industrial understanding based on fruit and vegetables; how are they transported, which are

most popular, which are cheaper – why, who/what determines price, where they come from etc.

41. Provide notices saying 'Hello' and 'Good-bye' in selected European languages. Devise activities for pupils to use these words.

42. Extend to everyday, simple phrases and structure in the form of a simple role drama.

43. Enter the number on a map of Europe of the main languages spoken from a numbered list.

44. Devise activities based on similarities and differences between the words for the numbers 1, 2, 3 in selected languages.

45. Identify the meaning of European road signs and symbols found in public places.

46. Invent symbols to protect the environment and assist others.

47. Make a collection of fairy tales, children's stories and legends from each European country.

48. Identify key festivals and holidays and place them on a year planner. Devise a class activity to take place on the days identified.

49. Collect pictures of national costumes from European and non-European nations.

50. Study the origins, customs and practices of the Olympic Games. Compare and contrast classical and modern forms.

51. Trace the origins of a variety of sports to specific nations.

52. Make historic buildings from junk materials, e.g. the Parthenon.

53. Study life in ancient times from the artifacts of selected countries, e.g. Greek vases.

54. Devise a number game using Roman numerals.

55. Make a selection of mosaics from different periods and countries. Devise art activities based on them.

56. Trace the development of the major world religions through the architectural forms of churches, mosques, cathedrals.

57. Identify countries that formed empires at different historical periods, e.g. Greek, Roman, Charlemagne, Napoleon, etc.

58. Trace the story of the voyages of discovery which linked Europe with the rest of the world.

59. Raise levels of civic and political awareness through accounts and pictures of both World Wars.

60. Devise a game based on a spinning disc divided into the 12 countries of the E.C.

61. Ditto using the names of countries in different languages.

62. Make cards with the names of the 12 E.C. countries and arrange them into the four main groups according to date of entry, e.g. Europe of the 6, 9, 10 and 12.

63. Collect political cartoons of major E.C. issues. Ask pupils to interpret them and devise their own caption.

64. Collect stamps from European countries.

65. Make a collection of stamps which have a commemorative theme or motif.

66. Design a European stamp to symbolise a chosen theme.

67. Investigate the logos and symbols of some European institutions: Council of Europe, E.C. European Movement, etc.

68. Write and perform a poem on the themes of co-operation, trust and friendship.

69. Make an anthology of poems on these and other relevant themes from different European and non-European countries. Compare and contrast them.

70. Devise activities based on the United Nations Declaration of Children's Rights of 20th November 1959, emphasising its global application.

71. Investigate dances in Europe, clapping, skipping in twos, in threes, in a circle. Organise parents and siblings to teach the children traditional dances from their country of origin.

72. Link flags with countries.

73. Make a domino game based on monuments and their location in selected cities.

74. Cut up a map of Europe. Invite the pupils to re-assemble the parts.

75. Create a breakfast, lunch and dinner menu. Enter on a map where the various foods came from. Identify the means by which the various goods were delivered.

76. Make a jigsaw puzzle from the map of Europe.

77. Make a work sheet to enter the cities and countries of Europe.

78. Devise activities based on airports, air routes and air lines. Pose travel questions for a variety of travellers and link with various subjects, e.g. maths, technology, history, etc.

79. Identify nationality plates on cars.

80. Make a map of the main waterways of Europe. Study the barge traffic and connecting shipping routes.

81. Connect capital cities with a map and unnamed photos.

82. Collect photos of children from different lands. Encourage their study by writing or telling stories about who they might be, what they might be doing or thinking.

83. Make a variety of quartet games, e.g. from stamps.

84. Match photos of major town mounted on cards with a named grid. Invite pupils to create a similar game.

85. Get your class to collect holiday postcards from various European destinations. Devise a game based on matching and identification.

86. Identify European place names in other countries of the world, e.g. London, Ohio, Copenhagen, New York, Paris, Illinois.

87. Devise a role play based on passports and customs and the advantages/disadvantages of controlled borders.

88. Identify specific delicacies from different regions in different countries.

89. Tell the story of where the name 'Europe' comes from. Take the starting point of the representation of a woman with a bull taken from contemporary or ancient illustrations. Make the link with other Greek legends. Take the alternative starting point of the Asian word 'Ereb' which means 'dark'. Viewed from Asia, Europe seems to be situated where the sun goes down therefore it is also named the 'evening country'. Trace connections between Asian and European trade routes.

90. Devise activities based on town twinning. Contact the local town twinning committee for support in developing exchanges/correspondence/joint planning of lessons.

91. Construct data sheets which combine key information about each European country by flag, car plate, name of country in three languages, land area, inhabitants in millions, population density, capital and large cities, etc.

92. Make a list of the main rivers in Europe. Devise a game which links them with their capital cities.

93. Trace rivers which flow through more than one country. Devise a game based on an historical journey along this river.

94. Devise a hexagonal puzzle based on rivers and mountain ranges. Mount on card. Cut up for re-assembly against a time check.

95. Calculate the length of major rivers.

96. Plot and record the height of major peaks in the seven main mountain ranges in Europe.

97. Which countries have no coasts?

98. Make a Euro-city train map of Europe.

99. Collect leaflets which show the railway network in selected European countries.

100. Devise a board or card game based on a journey through Europe using actual historical events.

101. Compile a Euro-quiz; the highest mountain, the largest town, the smallest town, the most rain, the longest night, the longest river, the biggest lake, the oldest buildings, the hottest summer, the most fog, the largest island, the flattest country, the biggest glacier, the most densely populated, the biggest port, etc. Add further examples.

102. Modify the above in levels of difficulty by giving clues or multiple choice answers.

103. Devise a series of activities on nature and the environment.

104. Make a map showing the distribution of concentrations of types of the main trees, cork, chestnuts, olives, vines, pines, beeches. What uses do people make of them? How are they related to the economy of the country?

105. Ditto – migratory and indigenous birds.

106. Ditto – flowers/plants.

107. Ditto – animals.

108. Tell stories by authors in different parts of Europe.

109. Use a classroom corner for exhibition of items, resources, artifacts from European countries.

110. Invite children from different classes or siblings to recount a journey to another country. Select journeys that link Europe with the rest of the world.

111. Invite children to give an account of receiving visitors from other European and non-European countries.

112. Brainstorm the class with ideas about what 'Europe' is. Write the ideas on cards. Pin them on the wall. Make critical selections. Group, set and categorise them. Allow pupils to make choices by removing labels whilst they are under investigation and return them to the wall when complete.

113. Celebrate a European feast day or compile a festival through games, songs, dances, plays, exhibitions. Invite parents and friends to a school exhibition and assembly.

114. Make a video on: 'One day in the life of ......'. Exchange with a school in another country.

115. Designate certain days or half days to specific countries to re-create aspects of the culture. Raise and destroy stereotypes in the process.

116. Launch a 'Europe Around Us' I-spy game or treasure trail in the locality.

117. Invite groups of pupils to compile illustrated data sheets of countries and regions within countries for exchange with other pupils.

118. Invite pupils to compile a portfolio of writing, photos, illustrations, etc. to portray themselves to a link school elsewhere in Europe.

119. Computerise selected information on key themes and countries on a micro-computer database through pupil task groups.

120. Devise critical and analytical tasks on media reportage of a European issue: e.g. mount a debate and vote on the outcome.

121. Develop a peer tutor system to assist pupils with special needs.

Appendix 9: Useful addresses

Arion, Programme of Study Visits for Education Specialists, Short Courses and Study Visits Section, Central Bureau for Educational Visits and Exchanges, Seymour Mews House, Seymour Mews, London W1H 9PE.

Association for Language Learning, 16 Regent Place, Rugby CV23 2PN.

Association for Teacher Education in Europe, Rue de la Concorde 51, B-1050, Brussels, Belgium.

British Comparative and International Education Society, Department of Education, University of Cambridge, 17 Trumpington Street, Cambridge CB2 1QA.

Central Bureau for Educational Visits and Exchanges, Seymour Mews House, Seymour Mews, London, W1H 9PE.

Centre for Information on Language Teaching and Research, Regent's College, Inner Circle, Regent's Park, London NW1 4NS

Commission of the European Communities, 8 Storey's Gate, London, SW1P 3AT.

Council of Europe, School Education Division, BA431/R6, F-67006, Strasbourg Cedex.

Education Information Network in the European Community, Eurydice European Unit, N.F.E.R., The Mere Upton Park, Slough SL1 2DQ.

European Association of Teachers, 20 Brookfield, Highgate West Hill, London N6 6AS.

European Community Action Scheme for the Mobility of University Students, The University, Canterbury, Kent CT2 7PB.

European Cultural Foundation, County End, Bushey Heath, London WD2 1NY.

European Movement, Europe House, 1 Whitehall Place, London SW1A 2HA.

European Parliament Information Office, 2 Queen Anne's Gate, London SW1A 9AA.

Friends Around the World Project, Sheffield Education Computing Centre, 20 Union Road, Sheffield S11 9EF.

Geographical Association, 341 Fulwood Road, Fulwood, Sheffield S10 3BP.

Historical Association, 59 Kennington Park Road, London SE11 4JH.

Nottingham Polytechnic Centre for European Education, Faculty of Education, Clifton Hall, Clifton Village, Nottingham NG11 8NS.

Politics Association, 16 Gower Street, London WC1E 6DP.

U.K. Centre for European Education, Seymour Mews House, Seymour Mews, London W1H 9PE.

U.K. Lingua Unit, Seymour Mews House, Seymour Mews, London W1H 9PE.

Youth Exchanges in the European Community, Youth Exchange Centre, Seymour Mews House, Seymour Mews, London W1H 9PE.

Bibliography

Antonouris, G. (1990) *The European Dimension in Teacher Training Activity Books 1 and 2*. Faculty of Education, Nottingham Polytechnic.

Antonouris, G. and Wilson, J. (1989) *Equal Opportunities in Schools: New Dimensions in Topic Work*. London: Cassell.

Austin, R. (1990) *Communicating Across Europe*. Belfast: European Studies Project.

Ball, S. J. (ed.) (1990) *Foucault and Education: Disciplines and Knowledge*. London and New York: Routledge.

Beddis, R. and Mares, C. (1988) *School Links International: A New Approach to Primary School Linking Around the World*. Avon County Council/Tidy Britain Group.

Bell, G. H. (1985) 'Can schools develop knowledge of their practice?' *School Organisation*, Vol. 5 No. 2 pp. 176–84.

Bell, G. H. (1987) 'Developing intercultural understanding: an action research approach', *School Organisation*, Vol. 7, pp. 272–9.

Bell, G. H. (1988) 'Using action inquiry', in J. Nias and S. Groundwater-Smith (eds) *The Enquiring Teacher: Supporting and Sustaining Teacher Research*, Lewes: The Falmer Press.

Bell, G. H. (1989a) 'Developing a European dimension of the teacher training curriculum, *European Journal of Teacher Education*, Vol. 12 No. 3 pp. 229–37.

Bell, G. H. (1989b) 'Europe in the primary school: a collaborative venture between schools and teacher trainers', *British Journal of In-Service Education*, Vol. 15 No. 2 pp. 86–94.

Bell, G. H. and Colbeck, B. (1989) *Experiencing Integration: The Sunnyside Action Inquiry Project*. Lewes: The Falmer Press.

Bell, G. H. and Dennis, S. (1991) 'Special needs development, networking and managing for change', *European Journal of Special Needs Education*, Vol. 6 No. 2 pp. 133–46.

Bell, G. H. and Lloyd, J. T. (1989) *Europe in the Primary School: A Case Review Report*. Sheffield: PAVIC Publications.

Bell, G. H., Miles, A. G. and Ovens, P. (1989) *Europe in the Primary School in England: A Case Study*. Sheffield: PAVIC Publications.

177

Bell, G.H. and Pennington, R.C. (1981) 'Network of European teacher education: proceedings of an inaugural conference, Antwerp, 1979', *Collected Original Resources in Education*, Vol. 5.

Bell, G.H. and Pennington, R.C. (1988) 'The role of consultants and facilitators in school based enquiry', *Collected Original Resources in Education*, Vol. 12 No. 3 October.

Bennis, W.G. (1976) *The Planning of Change* (3rd edn). New York: Holt, Reinhart and Winston.

Bridges, D. (ed.) (1978) 'Political education, Cambridge', *Journal of Education*, Vol. 8 Nos. 2 and 3.

Calogiannakis-Hourdakis, P. (1988) 'Le Role de Communautes D'Eleves dans La Socialisation Politique des Lyceens en Grece'. PhD. Thesis, Academie de Paris, Sorbonne, France.

Carr, W. and Kemmis, S. (1986) *Becoming Critical: Education, Knowledge and Action Research*. Lewes: The Falmer Press.

Carrington, B. and Short, G. (1987) 'Breakthrough to political literacy: political education, anti-racist teaching and the primary school', *Journal of Educational Policy*, Vol. 2 No. 1 pp. 1–13.

Central Bureau for Educational Visits and Exchanges (1990) *European Awareness Pilot Project*. London: Central Bureau.

Centre for Educational Research and Innovation (1989) *One School, Many Cultures*. Paris, O.E.C.D.

C.E.V.N.O. (1987) *The European Dimension in Education: Report of the European Conference*, Maastricht, Netherlands, June 18–20, 1987, Alkmaar.

Commission of the European Communities (1987) *Greater Emphasis for the* of Ministers of Education meeting within the Council, December 13th, 1976, Official Journal, December 20th, para. iv, Section 5.

Commission of the European Communities (1988) Resolution of the Council and the Ministers of Education meeting within the Council on the European Dimension in Education, 24th May, Official Journal 88/C/177/02.

Commission of the European Communities (1988) *Jean Monnet, A Grand Design for Europe*, Luxembourg, Brussels: Office for Official Publications of the European Communities.

Commission of the European Communities (1989) *Guide to the European Community Programmes in the Fields of Education, Training and Youth*. Task Force: Human Resources, Education, Training and Youth. Brussels, Eurydice.

Commission of the European Communities (1989) *Greater Emphasis for the European Dimension in Education*. Brussels: Commission of the European Communities.

Convey, A. (ed.) (1988) *Teacher Training and 1992*. London: U.K. Centre for European Education.

Council of Europe (1982) *Contribution to the Development of a New Education Policy*. Strasbourg, Council of Europe.

Council of Europe (1984) *Learning for Life*. Strasbourg, Council of Europe.

Council of Europe (1989) *Using the New Technologies to Create Links Between Schools Throughout the World*. Strasbourg, Council of Europe.

178

Couzens Hoy, D. (ed.) (1986) *Foucault: A Critical Reader*. Oxford: Basil Blackwell.

Crick, B. and Porter, A. (eds) (1978) *Political Education and Political Literacy*. London: Longman.

Department of Education and Science (1986) *Geography from 5-16: Curriculum Matters 7*. London: H.M.S.O.

Department of Education and Science (1989) *Initial Teacher Training: Approval of Courses*. Circular 24/89, 10th November, D.E.S.

Department of Education and Science (1989) *Planning for School Development: Advice to Governors, Headteachers and Teachers*. London: D.E.S.

Department of Education and Science (1991) *The Objectives of the European Dimension in Education*. London: D.E.S.

Doncaster L. E. A./Nottingham Polytechnic, Faculty of Education (1990) *The European Dimension in the Primary School Curriculum: Vol. 1 Reports. Vol.2 Appendices (mimeo)*.

Elliott, G. (1980) *Self Evaluation and the Teacher: An Annotated Bibliography and Report on Current Practice*. Parts 1 and 2. London: Schools Council.

Elliott, J. (1975) in D. Bridges and P. Scrimshaw (eds) *Values and Authority in Schools*. London: Hodder & Stoughton.

Elliott, J. (1978) 'What is action research in schools?' Journal of Curriculum *Studies*, Vol. 11 No. 2 pp. 355-7.

Elliott, J. (1991) *Action Research for Educational Change*. Milton Keynes: Open University Press.

Elliott, R. K. (1974) 'Education, Love of One's Subject and the Love of Truth', Proceedings of the Philosophy of Education Society for Great Britain. Vol. viii. No. 1 pp. 135-53.

Elliott-Kemp, J. and Williams, G. L. (1980) *Diagnosis of Individual and Organisational Needs in Schools*. Sheffield: PAVIC Publication, Sheffield City Polytechnic.

European Dimension in Teaching (1991) *Europe: Its Place in the World*. London: U.K. Centre for European Education.

European Parents Association (1988) *The European Dimension in Education: The Parental Contribution Towards 1992*. Brussels: E.P.A.

European Parents Association (1990) *Special Bulletin*. Brussels: E.P.A.

Flouris, G. and Spiridakis, J. (1988) *Political Socialisation and the World Citizen*. Paper presented to the Seventeenth International Conference on the Unity of the Sciences, Los Angeles, California, Nov. 24-7 (mimeo).

Fogelman, K. (1990) *Citizenship in Secondary Schools: A National Survey in 'Encouraging Citizenship'*, London: H.M.S.O.

Foucault, M. (1970) *The Order of Things: An Archaeology of the Human Sciences*. London: Tavistock Publications.

Foucault, M. (trans. A. Sheridan) (1977) *Discipline and Punish*. Harmondsworth: Penguin.

Fountain, S. and Selby, D. (1988) 'Global education in the primary school', *Aspects of Education*, Vol. 38 pp. 21-42.

Fullan, M. G. (1982) *The Meaning of Educational Change*. New York: Teachers College Press.

Fullan, M. G. (1986) 'Improving the Implementation of Educational Change', *School Organisation*, Vol. 6, pp. 321–6.

Galesloot, L. and Ten Brinke, J. S. (1989) *Europe in the Primary School in Holland: The Utrecht Case Study*, Sheffield: PAVIC Publications.

Galton, M. and Blyth, A. (1989) *Handbook of Primary Education in Europe*. London: David Fulton.

Garcon, A. M. and Prat, R. (1990) *Europe in the Primary School in France: The Nancy Case Study*. Sheffield: PAVIC Publications.

Glaser, B. and Strauss, A. L. (1967) *The Discovery of Grounded Theory*. Chicago: Aldine.

Goodson, I. (1982) European co-operation in education: historical background and contemporary experience, *European Journal of Teacher Education*, Vol. 5 Nos. 1–2 pp. 1928.

Goodson, I. and McGivney, V. (1985) *European Dimensions and the Secondary School Curriculum*. Lewes: The Falmer Press.

Goodson, I., Oonk, H. and Scurati, C. (1984) *Curriculum Models on European Education*. Alkmaar: ECN Publication, No. 2.

Grant, N. (1973) *Problems of Cultural Identity in Europe – Participation and Identity*. Report of a Conference, 14–17 September. Comparative Education Society in Europe, British Section.

Grass, K., Heilig, B., Nehring, B. and Pommerenke, E. (1990) *Europe in the Primary School: The Schwäbisch-Gmünd Case Study*. Sheffield: PAVIC Publications.

Handy, C. (1977) 'The Organisation of Consent' in O. Boyd-Bennett *et al.* (eds) *Approaches to Post School Management*. London: Harper and Row, 1983.

Hellawell, D. E. (1986) 'Education for Intercultural Europeans', *Euro Education News*, 19, Supplement No. 1 February. U.K. Centre for European Education.

Her Majesty's Inspectorate (1989) *Aspects of Primary Education: The Teaching and Learning of History and Geography*. London: H.M.S.O.

Her Majesty's Stationery Office (1990) *Encouraging Citizenship: Report of the Commission on Citizenship*. London: H.M.S.O.

Hess, R. D. and Torney, J. V. (1965) *The Development of Basic Attitudes and Values Toward Government and Citizenship During the Elementary School Years*. Part 1. Co-operative Resource Project No. 1078): University of Chicago Press.

Hitchcock, G. and Hughes, D. (1989) *Research and the Teacher: A Qualitative Introduction to School Based Research*. London: Routledge.

Hudson, W. D. (1977) *Learning to be Rational*. Proceedings of the Philosophy of Education Society of Great Britain, Vol. xi.

Humberside County Council (1990) *European Awareness Project*. Hull: Humberside L.E.A. (mimeo).

I.L.E.A. (1982) *Keeping the School Under Review: The Primary School*. London: Inner London Education Authority.

Jones, H. C. (1990) 'Education and 1992', *National Union of Teachers Education Review*, Spring 1990, pp. 23–30.

Kasper, H. and Kullen, S. (1989) *Europa Kartei*. Heinsberg. Agentur Dieck.

Kasper, H., Kullen, S. and Maier, I. (1990) *Europe in the Primary School in West Germany: The Reutlingen Case Study*. Sheffield: PAVIC Publications.

Koble, H. and Kullen, S. (1990) *Projekt Europe in der Primarstufe*. Horneburg, Verlag Sigrid Persen.

Kohnstamm, M. (1981) *Jean Monnet: The Power of the Imagination*. Florence. European University Institute.

Koval-Gillard, M. J. (1990) *Europe in the Primary School in Belgium: The Mons Case Study*. Sheffield. PAVIC Publications.

Lambert, W. E. and Klineberg, O. (1967) *Children's Views of Foreign Peoples*. New York: Appleton-Century-Crofts.

Langeveld, W. (1979) *Political Education for Teenagers*. Strasbourg, Council of Europe.

Letiche, H. K. (1990) *Europe in the Primary School in Holland: The Amsterdam Case Study*. Sheffield: PAVIC Publications.

Lewin, K. (1964) 'Action research and minority problems', *Journal of Social Issues*, 2, pp. 34–46.

Lewin, K. (1964) 'Group dynamics and social change' in A. Etzioni and E. Etzioni (eds) *Social Change*. New York: Basic Books.

Lynch, J. (1989) *Multicultural Education in a Global Society*. Lewes: The Falmer Press.

Macbeth, A. M. (1989) *Involving Parents: Effective Parent–Teacher Relations*. Oxford: Heinemann.

Macbeth, A. M., Corner, T., Nisbet, S., Nisbet, A., Ryan, D. and Strachan, D. (1984) *The Child Between: A Report on School-Family Relations in the Countries of the European Community*. Commission of the European Communities, Studies Collection, Education Series, Brussels, Commission of the European Communities.

McCarthy, T. (1978) *The Critical Theory of Jurgen Habermas*. London: Hutchinson.

Macdonald, B. (1977) 'A political classification of evaluation studies', in D. Hamilton *et al*. *Beyond the Numbers Game*. London: Macmillan.

McLean, M. (1990) *Britain and A Single Market Europe: Prospects for a Common School Curriculum*. London: Kogan Page.

McPeck, J. E. (1981) *Critical Thinking and Education*. Oxford: Martin Robertson.

Mangan, J. A. (ed.) (1990) *Making Imperial Mentalities: Socialisation and British Imperialism*. Manchester: Manchester University Press.

Mares, C. (ed.) (1985) *Our Europe: Environmental Awareness and Language Development through School Exchanges*. Brighton: Keep Britain Tidy Group.

Massialas, B. G. (ed.) (1972) *Political Youth, Traditional Schools*. Englewood Cliffs, N.J.: Prentice Hall.

Mickel, W. W. (1986) *The European Dimension in the Classroom: Justification, Documents and Proposals*. Alkmaar. European Curriculum Network Series No. 4.

Monnet, J. (trans. Richard Mayne) (1978) *Memoirs*. London: Collins.

National Curriculum Council (1990a) *The Whole Curriculum: Curriculum Guidance 3*. York: N.C.C.

National Curriculum Council (1990b) *Education for Economic and Industrial Understanding: Curriculum Guidance 4*. York: N.C.C.

National Curriculum Council (1990c) *Environmental Education: Curriculum Guidance 7*. York: N.C.C.

National Curriculum Council (1990d) *Education for Citizenship: Curriculum Guidance 8*. York: N.C.C.

National Curriculum Council (1990e) Report of Sub-Task Group on the European dimension in education, November.

Neave, G. (1984) *The E.E.C. and Education*. Stoke-on-Trent: Trentham Books.

Nias, J. and Groundwater-Smith, S. (eds) (1988) *The Enquiring Teacher: Supporting and Sustaining Teacher Research*. Lewes: The Falmer Press.

Oja, S. N. and Smulyan, L. (1989) *Collaborative Action Research: A Developmental Approach*. Lewes: The Falmer Press.

O'Neil, M. J. (1981) 'Nominal Group Technique. An evaluation data collection process', Society for Research into Higher Education. *Evaluation Newsletter*, 5, pp. 44–60.

O'Neil, M. J. and Jackson, L. (1983) *Nominal Group Technique: A Process for Initiating Curriculum Development in Higher Education*. Vol. 8 No. 2, pp. 129–38.

Peters, R. S. (1973) *Reason and Compassion*. London: Routledge & Kegan Paul.

Ryba, R. (1989) *National Policies for the European Dimension in Education in Actes de Palerme*, Association for Teacher Education in Europe. Paris: Hatier.

Scurati, C. (1989) *Europe in the Primary School in Italy: A Case Study*. Sheffield: PAVIC Publications.

Sheffield L.E.A. (1990a) *The European Dimension Statement*. Sheffield.

Sheffield L.E.A. (1990) *Sheffield European Dimension INSET Project*. Sheffield.

Sheridan, A. (1980) *Michel Foucault: The Will to Truth*. London: Tavistock.

Simons, H. (1987) *Getting to Know Schools in a Democracy: The Politics and Process of Evaluation*. Lewes: The Falmer Press.

Singh, B. R. (1989) 'Neutrality and commitment in teaching moral and social issues in a multicultural society', *Educational Review*. Vol. 41 No. 3 pp. 227–42.

Standing Conference of the Ministers of Education and Cultural Affairs of the Lander of the Federal Republic of Germany (1990) *Europe in the Classroom*. Bonn, Germany.

Stenhouse, L. (1969) 'Open minded teaching', *New Society*, 24 July.

Stenhouse, L. (1979) 'Case study in comparative education: particularity and generalisation', *Comparative Education*, 15, pp. 5–10.

Stenhouse, L. (1983) *Authority, Education and Emancipation*. London: Heinemann.

Stobart, M. (1990) Paper presented to the 12th National Conference of the U.K. Centre for European Education, London, 6th November (mimeo).

U.K. Centre for European Education (1989) *Resources for Teaching About Europe*. London: Central Bureau.

U.N.E.S.C.O. (1986) *International Understanding at School*, Special Supplement Part 1. U.N.E.S.C.O. pp. 33–8.

Vaniscotte, F. (1989) *70 Millions d'Eleves: L'Europe de l'education*. Paris: Hatier.

Visalberghi, A. (1989) 'Links between peace education, Third World development problems and environmental and world citizenship', *Ricerca Educativa*, Vol. 3–4 pp. 37–46.

Webb, R. (ed.) (1990) *Practitioner Research in the Primary School*. Lewes: The Falmer Press.

Weigand, P. (1990) 'Does travel broaden the mind?' *Education* 3–13, October.

Whitehead, J. (1989) 'How do we improve research based professionalism in education?' *British Educational Research Journal*, Vol. 15 No. 1 pp. 3–17.

Wilson, J. and Cowell, B. (1982) 'Educational studies: a problem of finding common ground', *European Journal of Education*, Vol. 17 No. 4 pp. 425–31.

Winter, R. (1989) *Learning from Experience: Principles and Practice in Action Research*. Lewes: The Falmer Press.

Wolfendale, S. (ed.) (1989) *Parental Involvement: Developing Networks Between Schools, Home and Community*. London: Cassell.

Index